UNLIMITED MEMORY

TABLE OF CONTENTS

Chapter 1: INTRODUCTION

Do you ever wonder about the sages living alone in the mountains, and think, "I bet they can fill out a spreadsheet in no time!?"

Science indicates, somewhat unexpectedly, they could.

With the recent revival of Western mindfulness and meditation, we are beginning to become fully aware of the consequences of being completely conscious. What we find is that the knowledge is more than the paltry benefits of inner peace and real happiness: it's beneficial for business as well.

-- concentration, decreasing tension, and clearing the mind to make better decisions, many effective CEOs have already proved their strength. And now, we got the data to show that they are correct.

Mindfulness is hard to describe. The definition is, in essence, one of the triggers that some people are focusing on while trying to attain attention.

To boil it down, mindfulness is being especially conscious or conscious of what's going on in the present moment. And, contrary to common opinion, it's not something that just occurs while you're meditating — it's a state of mind that you should always embrace.

Perhaps it's easier to describe what knowledge isn't: being engulfed by distractions. Also, innocuous distractions (such as seeing a person walking past your desk) can stop you at the moment from living — or working. Some people are equating mindfulness to not thinking at all, but that's not accurate: distractions are what's missing from your brain but not thoughts. If you are at work thinking, you should think about it too.

One final important element of conscientiousness is the focus on the resulting process. Part of being at the moment means completely committing to the task at hand, rather than dwelling on what the consequences will be (and how they will affect you). This naturally lends itself to profitability, because instead of worrying about the hypothetical future, you stay focused on your job.

Chapter 2: MINDFULNESS

What is Mindfulness?

Should you clear your mind, or concentrate on one thing? The Mindful Concept of Mindfulness is here.

Compassion. It is a really clear term. It suggests that the mind attends entirely to what is happening, to what you are doing, to the space in which you are going. That might sound trivial, except for the irritating fact that we so frequently veer from the matter. Our mind is escaping, we're losing contact with our bodies, and we're getting lost in obsessive thoughts about something that's just happening or thinking about the future very early. And that makes us worried.

Mindfulness is the basic human ability to be fully present, conscious of where we are and what we are doing and not overly reactive or overwhelmed by what is happening around us.

And no matter how far we float away, there is a sense of consciousness right there to snap us back to where we are and what we feel and do. If you want to know what knowledge is, try it for a while at first. Since it is difficult to nail down in words, in books, websites, audio, and video, you will find slight variations in the meaning.

The Definition of Mindfulness

Mindfulness is the basic human ability to be fully present, conscious of where we are and what we are doing and not overly reactive or overwhelmed by what is happening around us.

Mindfulness is a quality already possessed by any human being; it's not something you have to conjure up; you just have to know how to access it.

The Types of mindfulness practice

While it is innate to be mindful, it can be cultivated using proven techniques. Here are just a few examples:

1. Sitting, walking, standing and moving meditation (also it is possible to lie down but often leads to sleep);
2. We insert short pauses into everyday life;
3. Meditation exercise is mixed with other practices, such as yoga or sports.

Mindfulness Benefits Practice:

When we meditate, it doesn't help focus on the benefits, but only doing the practice, and yet there are advantages; otherwise, no one should do it.

When we are mindful, we reduce stress, improve performance, gain insight and awareness by observing one's mind, and increase our attention to the well-being of others.

Meditation on mindfulness offers us a moment in our lives where we can suspend judgment and unleash our innate curiosity about the workings of the mind, addressing our experience with comfort and kindness — to ourselves and others.

8 Facts About mindfulness:

1. mindfulness is neither mysterious nor exotic. We are familiar with it because it is what we are already doing, how we are already. It takes several types and goes by several names.

2. Mindfulness is not something we do particularly recently. We already have the opportunity to be there, and it does not demand that we alter who we are. But we can develop these inherent qualities with clear activities that are clinically established to benefit us, our loved ones, our friends and colleagues, the people with whom we interact and the institutions and organizations in which we engage

3. They don't have to adjust. Solutions that ask us to change who we are or to become something that we are not have repeatedly failed. Mindfulness recognizes and cultivates the best of people we are.

4. Mindfulness can become a global movement that is changing. It is for this reason:

5. Anybody can do it. The practice of mindfulness cultivates common human values and demands that none change their beliefs. Everyone can gain, and the learning is quick.

6. It is a way of life. Mindfulness is more than pure exercise. It adds understanding and compassion to all that we do — and it cuts down needless tension. Just a little does change our lives.

7. It's basing on facts. We don't have to take mindfulness to heart. Both science and experience show their positive health, happiness, work, and relationship benefits.

8. This is sparking creativity. As we deal with the growing complexities and uncertainty of our environment, being aware may lead us to efficient, resilient, low-cost solutions to seemingly intransigent issues.

Mindfulness is not in your head

If we think about mindfulness and meditation (with a capital M), we might get stuck on thinking about our thoughts: we're trying to do something about what's trying on in our minds. It's as if these bodies that we have are merely bulky bags for lugging around our minds.

Nevertheless, having it all remain in your head lacks a sense of good old gravity.

Meditation starts in the body and stops. This means taking the time to pay attention to where we are and what is happening, and this begins by becoming mindful of our body

The method will make things look floating — as if we don't have to walk around. Everything we can do is a wave.

Yet, in the body, meditation begins and stops. It involves taking the time to pay attention to where we are and what is going on, and that begins with our body being aware. The very act can be soothing, as our body has internal rhythms which help it to relax if we give it a chance.

How to Sit for Meditation

Here's a posture practice that can be used as the starting stage of a meditation practice period or simply as something to do for one minute, perhaps to stabilize yourself and find a moment of relaxation before going back into the fray. If you have injuries or other physical difficulties, this may be changed to suit your situation.

1. Take a seat. Whatever you sit on — a chair, a cushion for meditation, a park bench — find a spot that gives you a stable, solid seat that is not perching or hanging back.

2. Remember what they are doing with your hands. If you are on a couch on the floor, comfortably cross your legs in front of you. (If you're already doing some sort of seated yoga posture, go ahead.) If you're on a chair, it's ok if your feet's bottom touches the floor.

3. Straighten your upper body — but don't stiffen. The backbone is of natural curvature. Let's leave it there. The head and shoulders should rest comfortably on top of the vertebrae.

4. Place the upper arms parallel to the upper body. Then let your hands go down on your legs tops. Your hands land in the right position with your upper arms at your sides. They're going to make you hunch too far away. They're going to make you stiff too far out. You're tuning your body's strings – not too tight and not too loose.

5. Drop your chin a little, and let down your gaze gently. You could let lower your eyelids. When you feel the need, you can lower them down entirely, but when meditating, you do not need to close your eyes. You should only let what seems to be there before your eyes, without dwelling on it.

6. Be there for a couple of instants. Relax and unwind. Now get up and go about your day. And if the next thing on the list is to do some practice of mindfulness by paying attention to your breath or the sensations in your body, you've started on the right foot — and hands and arms and all the rest.

7. Turn on again. When your posture is set, feel your breath — or some people say "follow" it — as it goes out and as it goes in. (Some iterations of the practice put more focus on the outbreak, and you simply leave a spacious pause for the breath.) Eventually, your mind will leave your breath and drift to other areas.
8. When you get around to notice this — in a few seconds, a minute, five minutes — the breath returns your attention. Do not hesitate to judge yourself or get obsessed with the substance of the thoughts. Return. You are going abroad; you are coming back.
9. This is it. This is education. It has been said often that this is very simple, but it is not necessarily easy. The aim is just to keep on doing it. Tests are to accrue.

HOW MINDFULNESS AFFECTS THE BRAIN

Removing the mysticism, how does the mindfulness influence the brain exactly? Research has recorded the effectiveness of mindfulness in a wide variety of clinical applications, ranging from mental health interventions such as rehabilitation of PTSD to quantifiable improvements in how we feel about ourselves.

The beneficial results of mindfulness can be regarded as an ancient secret from prehistoric times. Still, it's only recently — thanks to the latest advances in MRI, EEG, and other brain-scanning technology — that we have been able to scientifically validate what the gurus have known for centuries.

For example, meditative activities — the mindfulness element that is easiest to study scientifically — reduce the number of beta waves in the brain, correlated with stress and anxiety, or strong rational thinking at low rates. So we may conclude immediately that mindfulness fulfills the promise of relaxation, just as it is marketed.

What we know, however, goes far deeper than that. A landmark 2005 research by Dr. Sara W. Lazar, et al., found that meditation in the prefrontal cortex significantly increases brain capacity. Although it is remarkable enough to essentially increase brain capacity, what is especially fascinating is that such improvements occur in the prefrontal cortex.

To oversimplify a complex topic, what distinguishes humans from animals is the prefrontal cortex. Not that animals do not have it, just that in humans, it is much more advanced. Most of our rational thought and reasoning is responsible for the prefrontal cortex, including empathy, self-awareness, perception, morality, and the ability to concentrate during emotional turmoil.

With that in mind, it's easy to see how mindfulness by training the right parts of your brain could increase your productivity. Let's take an individual look at each area.

Focus

A better prefrontal cortex gives you even the unproductive ones more control over your emotions. Research by the University of California found that just two weeks of carefulness training effectively "reduced mind wandering among participants who were vulnerable to pre-testing diversion," not to mention how it increased the GRE test scores of subjects.

Decision-Making

Since major decisions are made in the prefrontal cortex, it is fair that understanding can be a great help to make better choices.

Although quantifying and calculating is a difficult subject, what we know — thanks to a study by the University of Pennsylvania — is that being conscious mitigates the sunk cost bias. Meditation prevents the brain from making subjective decisions by stressing contextual relationships and providing a stronger and more rational perspective.

Relief from tension

Stress relief is justification enough for many people to dive into mindfulness. Although clinical evidence is somewhat irrelevant — you can only see for yourself how meditation relieves stress — a study by John Hopkins University concluded that "meditation programs can result in small to moderate reductions of multiple negative dimensions of psychological stress," as described in the paper as "anxiety, depression, and stress."

The effects of understanding stress management are directly relevant to business and profitability and have been recorded already.

By introducing a six-week course on mindfulness and cognitive behavioral therapy, Transport for London recorded 71 percent fewer days off due to stress, anxiety, or depression, and a 50 percent decrease in total absences. The participants have registered changes in their relationships (80%), the ability to relax more easily (79%), improved sleep habits (64%), and more workplace satisfaction (54%).

Relationships with colleagues

It's often taken for granted, particularly in business, that communication and teamwork are skills that can be learned, and some employees are better at them than others. While there have been no workplace-specific studies, a joint study by Harvard UniversityNortheastern University found that "meditation directly improved compassionate response" to people who needed support. Considering the connection to empathy in the prefrontal cortex, these findings are possibly just the tip of the iceberg.

Creative Problem Solving

It's interesting, for anything as ethereal as creativity, how much scientific evidence there shows its relation to mindfulness.

First, a study by Leiden University found that the effects of meditation on divergent thought are "robust." Divergent thinking is the process of generating many new and original concepts in comparison to convergent thinking, which is all about deducting a single inference from different inputs.

In addition to immediate outcomes, a report by the Fielding Graduate University has expanded on these findings to include increased innovation over the long term. This research also found that meditating participants were 121 percent more capable of building on other people's thoughts, harking back to the influence of mindfulness on empathy.

Experts also found out that mindfulness makes three of the four phases of the creative process easier:

1. Preparation — Enhanced, divergent thought generates more ideas to get started with.
2. Incubation — Awareness by-beta waves makes it easier to relax and briefly ignore a problem, an integral stage of the creative process. (This report describes the circumstances better.)

3. Illumination — More self-knowledge and comprehension of one's emotions enhances the link with the subconscious, making it easier for Eureka to come across moments.

The fourth level, testing, relies more on rational evaluation and fine-tuning of the idea; that kind of thought is outside the purview of consciousness.

Happiness

Can you bring happiness to a value? Yeah, and that worth is 12 percent, according to a report by the University of Warwick, that's how much more successful, happy workers are. Although a conservative estimate is 12 percent — some subjects have achieved efficiency as much as 20 percent higher than the control group.

We have already addressed how perception reduces tension, but a study by the Michigan University of North Carolina shows a more clear connection between meditation and positive emotions. If you are still unconvinced, simply ask Matthieu Ricard, the happiest person in the world as decided by brain scans. Ricard happens to be a Tibetan monk, who is no stranger to meditation and mindfulness.

The same study also found a strong connection between the time spent meditating and the "capacity for pleasure and a reduced tendency to depression" of an individual. Even subjects with "just three weeks of 20-minute meditation a day" found marginally better results than those who never meditated at all.

HOW TO ACHIEVE MINDFULNESS THROUGH MEDITATION

While consciousness is often referred to as a natural state, the reality is that achieving it is more like a skill: it needs to be mastered and fine-tuned before being used properly. In modern society, there is no lack of distractions, and it takes time to train yourself to block them out. Although some people have been active in studying mindfulness skills on their own, others are luckier to enter a group or research under an expert.

Since it takes practice and preparation to attain consciousness, the subject is closely linked to mediation, the most common (but not the only) form of achieving it.

Meditation is similarly difficult to explain — it's more like the lack of action than an act itself. Additionally, there are hundreds of different ways of meditating, from centuriesold Zen Buddhist practices to more recent Guided Meditations tailored for busier times.

The common thread in all mediation is the aim of drawing your attention to the perceptions of the present moment — that is, attaining consciousness. Guides allow meditators to observe but not engage with their thoughts. Methods differ but often include relying on the senses, like a gentle skin breeze.

You can also meditate on your breathing in the absence of other sensations; for instance, if you concentrate enough, you'll find the air is colder going into your nose and warmer going out. That's as good as any prompt to get you going.

Meditation makes some people think of monks sitting in an empty stone temple with their legs crossed, but it could just as well be you sitting at your desk and shutting your eyes for a few minutes. Call it whatever you want, but it's pretty clear to take a moment to calm down. You meditated all your life here and there without even knowing it.

5 WAYS TO SHOW MINDFULNESS AT WORK

1. Exercises of Meditation

Meditation does not need to be regimented or bullied. This can be done practically everywhere and anywhere, only by taking a few minutes to yourself. Here are tips for the beginner to meditate, for whenever you have some free time:

Get feeling relaxed. There's no need for you to sit upright and cross beamed to meditate. The most important thing is that you're relaxed, so if that's what's relaxing for you, feel free to meditate in a chair, lie in bed or even stand. The aim is to eliminate distractions, so find a place that you can hold without any problems.

Body check for stress. Beginning at the top of your head and heading down, note the stress, and relieve any points in your body. Your chin, your back, your neck, and sometimes even your jaw are the usual suspects.

Don't beat yourself for thinking. It's not easy, of course, to clear your mind of every thought. Don't get upset with yourself that you can't turn your mind off — it happens to everybody, including experts in meditation.

Just follow certain thoughts as your mind "floats by." One part of the cycle is to let them come and go. It always counts as meditating, as long as you don't touch them.

4-7-8 Respiratory procedure. For beginners who have trouble clearing their minds, here's a good method: concentrate on your breathing, specifically using the 4-7-8 technique:

- Four seconds to breathe in.
- Grant seven seconds to hold your breath.
- Exhale FOR 8 seconds.
- Repeat.

That's a nice meditation on "training wheels" for people struggling to be idle. The directions are sufficiently complex to keep the mind occupied with counting, but still sufficiently clear that they do not detract from being attentive.

If jumping in is still too hard, you can download a Meditation Aid app. Apps such as Relax and Wait, Breathe & Think serve as automatic teachers. These apps offer enough versatility to satisfy you as you move, with separate, voice-guided meditations at different time intervals.

2. Avoid Multitasking

Multitasking is what you could term a "false friend" — it makes you feel like you're more successful, but the final result isn't as nice as you think, as an Ohio State study demonstrates.

Everything that multitasking does is water down the efforts for each task, rather than adding full attention to each task. However, doing one task at a time helps to practice your concentration, suit your mindfulness with hand-and-hand.

Zapier comes in handy here. You can easily program menial tasks as an automation device to complete automatically — the same kinds of tasks that are tempting to do with multitasking because they seem tiny and brainless.

3. Adopt a Mindset of Growth

Stanford Psychology Department Dr. Carol Dweck argues that there are two forms of mentality: set, and development. A fixed outlook treats personality characteristics, abilities, and gifts as immutable and unchangeable. An attitude of development recognizes that certain aspects can be modified, educated, and strengthened.

Based on the statistical evidence we discussed this entire essay, an attitude of development is closer to reality: the data indicates that the characteristics of people have changed unambiguously and that certain abilities have developed. If you want the same good outcomes, then it starts with believing that you will get them.

And research by Dweck has also confirmed the positive effects of a business attitude on production.

4. Stick to the Practices

You have to practice it daily to get the most out of your mindfulness. For beginners, the best advice is to meditate at least once a day and make it a routine. Only twenty minutes a day, as we heard from the UNC-UM study above, will yield measurable results in just three weeks.

The true amount of time might be even lower: Dr. Sara Lazar, the Harvard neuroscientist behind the discovery that perception improves prefrontal cortex density, acknowledged in an interview that "student anecdotal reports indicate that 10 minutes a day may have some subjective value," but that "we need to check it out." Of course, the more you practice each session, the more you can get back.

Regular meditation doesn't have to take a long time, but when you start, the problem is less about the dedication to time and more about remembering to do it every day.

Set an alert reminder during the first few days, so that you don't forget. Whatever time of day is perfect for you, you can choose as long as you do it.

5. Professional Direction

Are you involved in all of the organization's mindfulness training? Having a person to accept conscientiousness seems simple compared to getting a community of people on board. However, you can still enlist the assistance of experts or agencies to enforce it around the business.

There are plenty of workshops to teach entrepreneurial mindfulness. Check for groups under MBSR (Mindfulness-Based Stress Relief) or MBCT (Mindfulness-Based Cognitive Training), with most courses of four to eight weeks duration. Alternatively, if you are using an online course or webinar, you don't need an in-house teacher. For logistics, they are more versatile and can deliver the same level of instruction.

The Insight Timer mindfulness app encourages contact with the world of meditation and can help you find the right guides or mentors. You can find teachers in your field, or simply follow the advice you find there on your own.

When you're very serious about optimizing your productivity — not to mention something about enhancing your life and happiness — consciousness isn't anything to shrug off. At first, it

might seem soft, but with evidence confirming its results, it's
worth trying out for yourself or your entire team.

Chapter 3: BEING MINDFUL: FREE YOURSELF FROM NEGATIVE THOUGHT

The avoidance of negative feelings is one of the first steps to be taken to build knowledge both at work and at home. The next time you get worried about an on-the-job deadline or a personal financial problem, note the thoughts you start having. Can you tell yourself to take a break, and you're going to have it done on time? Likely not. On the other hand, will you start worrying instantly that you are not going to finish the project on time? If you're like other people, your mind is likely to leap to the worst conclusions that include anything, including being shot, being homeless, not paying a bill on time.

There is no place for these kinds of negative thinking, and there are many tips and tricks to help you get through this damaging line of thought.

Be Free from Negative Thoughts

It's time to finally take control of your life and your thoughts. It's going to be a beautiful transformation you won't believe until you see it firsthand—one of the most exhilarating feelings ever to be free from negative thought. Life is stressful enough already, so why would you like to add to that? You, and you alone, have it inside you to drive those negative feelings out of existence forever. Falling into this poor habit is easy, but getting rid of these feelings is not easy.

It takes a lot of effort and intense mind and body discipline, but once you practice this new way of thinking constantly, it will be easier to keep the negative thoughts out of your head. You'll soon learn to make this a habit, and it'll change all aspects of your life completely.

What is the number one way of fighting off this way of thinking? Compassion! Being aware can help in so many areas of your life, especially in the workplace. You have to smash the turmoil inside of your mind and just try to be in the moment. Everything you need to do tomorrow will be there, and you'll get it done. Remember that yesterday is gone, and tomorrow is not yet here. Keep living in the present and, in all aspects of your life, you are one step closer to a less stressful life.

The Effect of Stress on Health

Stress can have a crippling effect both on your physical and mental health. "Stress is the body's reaction to any shift that needs alteration or response," according to WebMD. The Occupational Safety and Health Administration (OSHA) recently declared stress as an occupational threat that costs the American economy more than $300 billion annually. (WebMD, 2012) Here are only a few stress symptoms which you should be searching for:

- Headache
- Stomach issues
- Insomnia
- Muscle tension
- Chest pain
- Fatigue

- Anxiety
- Depression
- Lack of motivation
- Loss of interest
- Abusing things such as alcohol, drugs, or even food
- Moodiness
- Irritability

All the symptoms mentioned above might not sound like such a big deal if you encounter them over the year intermittently, but after a while, they will hurt your quality of life. Such issues can also cause more severe health conditions, such as high blood pressure, obesity, heart disease, or misuse of drugs. (www.mayoclinic.org, 2013) Stress has a very serious effect on your physical and emotional well-being and is not meant to be taken lightly. Now is the time to smash your life's turmoil and start living your life at the moment, free of tension. When you can achieve, it is an attainable objective.

THE RELATIONSHIP BETWEEN MIND AND BODY

There is a clear link between your mind and your body, without a doubt. Carefulness will bind your mind and body and will allow you to cope with daily stresses better. When you're on the road to teaching yourself to be more mindful and aware of the moment, you're going to be shocked how quickly you're going to get through the day and become a more productive and less depressed individual at home and at work, which is what everybody is aiming towards.

Living in the moment is incredibly necessary and not thinking about yesterday or tomorrow. You will need to commit to making a shift, and while it's not going to be easy at first, if you stick with it and don't give up, you will see results. Just make sure to keep yourself isolated from your feelings. For example, each time you find a negative thought trying to make its way into your mind, try to force the thought out of your head by replacing it with a positive thought immediately. It will be a relentless fight for you in the beginning, but it's a war that certainly can be won.

Mindfulness is all about preparing the mind to think differently, and that's what will significantly strengthen the link between mind and body.

Tips and tricks

There are also useful tips and tricks to remember when attempting to defeat negative thoughts. Below are only a couple to remember:

- Make some negative feelings written down. Take the time to write down all of your negative feelings. You should then take this piece of paper and either throw it away or tear it out.
- Ask yourself questions about each of those feelings. The second you hear a negative thought comes into your brain; you should ask yourself a few questions, like 1) Is it helpful to think? 2) Is the reflection true? And 3) Is it necessary to think? This will help you get a stronger perspective on these kinds of concepts. (Markway, Barbara, 2013)
- Exercising. Physical exercise is a perfect way to keep yourself balanced and to help circulate positive thoughts. For people everywhere, this is a major stress reliever. This will pump endorphins into your body and make you feel amazing.

- Just breathe. Only a moment will do wonders to quiet the mind with some deep breaths. Take the time to close your eyes and take a deep breath by concentrating only on your breathing. You can do this up to five minutes each day, several times a day.

One of the first things to concentrate on is to liberate one's self from negative thought. Keep on practicing, and negative thoughts should be a thing of the past before you know it. Although it's going to be something you have to focus on for the rest of your life, do know the more you practice this way of thinking, the more successful you're going to be in winning the battle.

Nearly 30,000 students study in the UK. It is revealed that dwelling on stressful life events could be the primary indicator of some of the most common health conditions of today. Results from this broad study showed that it's not only about events in life, but how we respond to certain events that form our psychological well-being.

If we agree that you can not regulate your thoughts or emotions, but rather concentrate on maintaining your understanding of them and controlling their effects, without getting caught up in them, then life can be much less stressful. The main thing is to understand that it is less main for the substance of our thoughts and feelings than how we let them affect us.

In reality, research shows that when individuals are told not to think about a particular thing, it makes it harder to get the thing out of their mind. But a frequent reexamination of negative emotions, also known as rumination, may be uncomfortable and counterproductive. It can, in some cases, lead to severe anxiety or persistent depression.

"It's like a groove pin," says Guy Winch, Ph.D., psychologist and author of Emotional
First Aid: Practical Methods to Treat Deficiencies, Rejection, Guilt, and Other Everyday Psychological Injuries. "When the groove gets deeper and deeper, the needle comes out of the groove a harder time."

This is where the training comes in. According to Jon Kabat-Zinn, a pioneer in mindfulness practices, it can be described as "to pay attention in a specific way, intentionally, in the present moment, and without judgment." In other words, mindfulness helps us to become more conscious of our thoughts without marking or judging them.

A review of the literature on attentiveness showed that cognitive-behavioral strategies focused on attentiveness are effective in minimizing both rumination and concern.

The researchers conclude, "Treatments in which participants are motivated to change their thought style, or to disengage from emotional reactions to rumination and/or anxiety, tend to be beneficial more generally."

Researchers Rimma Teper and her colleagues at the University of Toronto found that given the belief that meditation "empties the mind of emotions," mindfulness simply "allows us to become more conscious of and embrace emotional messages that help us regulate our behavior." Norman Farb and colleagues found mindfulness strategies facilitated the increased acceptance of negative emotions and improved behavior.

R. Chambers and colleagues concluded, based on an integrative analysis, that careful emotional control "does not entail repression of the emotional experience ... but requires comprehensive retraining of perception and non-reactivity, leading to the distortion of what is felt and enabling the person to select more actively those thoughts, emotions, and sensations with which they would associate,

So here are seven techniques of mindfulness which can help control negative thoughts and emotions:

1. Switch toward your approval, and not away from your negative thoughts or emotions. Note where you felt it in your body, and what emotion emerges with the physical sensation, until you become conscious of the negative thought or emotion. Only sit down with the emotion (e.g., anxiety, fear, rage, guilt) and don't deny it, or try to block or force it out. Become your expert observer.

2. Identify the thinking or feeling you feel and mark it. There are two aspects to this. The first is to mark it appropriately, and the second is how you say it. Use an observer's language is more effective than customizing it. Saying, "Yeah, this is fear that emerges in me right now," for instance, is preferable to "I am terrified."

3. See your feelings or emotions as transitory or temporary. If you want to hang onto them and get some form of incentive for doing so, they'll leave. Having the thought or emotion as a floating cloud or constantly asking yourself, "What is this thought/emotion now? "It's good.

4. Let go of having to control your feelings or thoughts. Stifling, suppressing, or ignoring thoughts and feelings in an attempt to retain power is not the same as emotional regulation. You are always being mindful of maintaining a balanced detachment.

5. Learn how to understand cognitive distortions; that is, accept the patterns of thinking that distort reality. Sources of cognitive distortions include prejudice in verifying, catastrophizing, personalizing, manipulating error, accusing, and the infamous "tyranny of ought." Understanding these biases and being a victim of them at the moment is practicing conscientiousness. It is, of course, important that sufficient action is taken afterward

6. Have a daily or weekly scheme for the time of negative thought or anger. It gives yourself permission to think or feel the negative thought or emotion briefly, but adhere to a fair limited time limit. So writing them down helps too.

7. Remember to breathe, pause, and respond, rather than react deliberately. If there are negative thoughts or feelings, we may either ruminate on them unnecessarily or respond impulsively. Mindfulness helps us to concentrate on our breathing, pause, and wait until we have put the techniques into practice and then respond deliberately with effective action.

Chapter 4: ENHANCING CONCENTRATION AND FOCUS WITH MINDFULNESS MEDITATION

It's hard to even have time for meals in our stressed out and busy world, far less time to meditate.

Yet here's the good news: you can spend just 10 minutes a day practicing meditation on mindfulness while still reap its benefits.

Adam Moore and his colleagues at the University of Liverpool John Moores in the UK found that practicing mindfulness meditation in brief regular intervals can positively affect and boost our concentration levels.

The researchers recruited 40 healthy adults, who were then assigned randomly to a group of meditation or a waitlist control group (age and gender were balanced between groups) to examine whether concentration can only be improved by the moderate practice of mindfulness.

Throughout 16 weeks, meditation group participants were given clear, mindful breathing exercises, and a total of ten minutes of meditation every day was observed, at least five days a week. Every participant held a meditation log, and each week recorded their frequency and period of practice.

Next, during the study, the researchers evaluated participants at three separate stages, using a combination of self-report questionnaires and a tandem Stroop task provided with an EEG monitor. The challenge consisted of four-color words displayed both in the same color as the written word (i.e., red, blue, green), and in different colors (i.e., red, blue, green); participants defined each word's color as easily and accurately as they could.

Here's what they did find.

I am practicing mindfulness meditation daily, even in brief intervals, dramatically impacted brain functions relevant to Stroop task success.

To put it another way: the research has shown that a very manageable routine of meditation – just ten minutes a day – is adequate to increase our attention and concentration.

What's more, the findings demonstrated how skills that we build and sharpen during the practice of mindfulness would support us in our daily lives.

One flaw to note – and recognized by the researchers – is the general imperfection of waitlist controls, and we would like to be careful in assuming that any of these results were triggered purely by the practices of mindfulness meditation.

MINDFULNESS ESTABLISHES NEW BRAIN CONNECTIONS

Mindfulness helps us develop new neural networks within the brain. Through neural networks, the brain is ultimately rewired to find different and creative ways to manage tasks and cope with stress and emotions. You are also helping increase the attention on yourself.

Research has shown that practicing mindfulness raises grey matter within the brain. Grey matter houses much of the brain cells as opposed to other brain structures. An increase in density may result in improved contact between the cells, and an increase in two areas known as the pons and raphe nucleus may enhance our overall psychological health.

Mindfulness-Based Stress Management

New research on meditation on mindfulness found that participants felt less psychological stress from anxiety, depression, and pain. That makes sense to me because when we feel anxiety, we appear to give too much power to our thoughts. Our emotions are running our lives, and it is frustrating when they are negative.

Strengthen your Concentration in 8 Weeks

Research performed at Massachusetts General Hospital was the first to identify density changes in the grey brain matter. Participants had decreased density in the brain areas responsible for: In as little as eight weeks.

- The mechanisms of thinking and memory
- Mental salience (some positive emotions are given top priority)
- Being able to consider multiple views
- Regulating emotions

Such brain regions are called the posterior cingulate, the temporoparietal lobe, the hippocampus, and the cerebellum.

While work continues, increases in the density of grey matter in different brain structures show potential for positive brain changes.

Such improvements can help to improve your concentration and allow you to remember more clearly what you are reading. Practicing mindfulness to a greater degree will help you take more control over what you're thinking about, creating more room for learning new things, understanding what you've already read, and that long-term memory.

New To Meditation?

Of the research participants mentioned above, they have all been new to meditation. This means after several weeks, everyone will start to experience the benefits.

You might think at first that your practice is distracting you more. That's because you're getting more understanding of everything, particularly distractions. You will encounter more thoughts as you learn to concentrate and focus on your heart, as you are aware of them. So during this time, it might feel like a thousand things are coming to you. .So this ensures that your concentration works better — you can find how quickly you can stop yourself from just sitting and looking at the wall

Consider needing to drive to work. It's a pretty familiar path, and every day you know what to expect. You'll see the same trees, signs, highways, and paths. So functions the brain. The more you think about it, the more embedded it is in your memory, the more you don't know any other way. The more you're used to wild, chaotic impulses, the more aware you'll need to be to stop them.

WAY TO MEDITATE

There are several ways of meditating on mindfulness: relaxation exercises, visualizations, and more. In my book I wrote earlier this year, you can find some — Why Mental Breaks Are Necessary — and here are a few more:

1. 60 Seconds — Take 60 seconds to concentrate on just breathing, nothing else. Perform several times a day. You may increase this length slowly over time, or simply double it every day. Don't think if you start worrying and don't concentrate on your breath, you failed. Being able to have one minute of warning, direct focus takes years of practice.

2. Conscious Observation — Choose an object, and devote all your attention to it. Do not research or evaluate it — just watch it for what it is. It could be a marker, a cup, a Penn State T-Shirt, or a wall mark. Practicing this is important because it gives you a sense of alertness, "awake," and places you in the present moment. Remember how, during this exercise, you are not worried about the past or the future.

3. Slowly Count to 10 — Count to 10 in your mind and catch yourself to see if you're worried about something you need to do, a thought from the past, a story you've made, or just trying to count it all. When you say to yourself, start over. You can start doing that a couple of times before you feel comfortable meditating.

4. Eat Slowly — Masters of Buddhism and Zen fall completely into the present moment by feeding gradually. This is a philosophy which they have taught for a very long time. Careful eating will slow down your meal and make you better appreciate the food that you have before you. Pay careful attention to the taste, the smell, the look of

the food. You may repeat affirmations like "I am thankful to be enjoying this wonderful meal" in your head.

3 STRATEGIES OF MEDITATION TO INCREASE FOCUS

1. Mindfulness

Among the many readily available meditation methods, the practice of mindfulness is one of the most common and well-known ways to enhance focus. Do you think of any mission that can be carried out perfectly without your full attention to it? Many activity involve high levels of focus, including driving, playing sports or music, reading, and paying attention to work or school. Therefore, you are more likely to gain gratification from homing in and accomplishing one mission you have selected than from attempting to juggle many at one go.

When you train the mind to stay present and completely concentrated on one topic-for example, physical stimuli or the breathing cycle-you also learn to let go of all other thoughts and distractions.

By finding that you don't have to pay attention to every little thing that pops into your mind, there is a lot of independence. Your capacity to focus naturally improves when you can be conscious at will.

2. Meditating Zen

An Italian neuroscientist named Giuseppe Pagnoni performed a study in which he compared the brain functions of a dozen long-term Zen meditation practitioners and a dozen similarly profiled individuals who were not familiar with meditation. Pagnoni found, according to an article in Psychology Today, that the minds of the meditators were more stable than those of the other group, and that their ability to focus was superior. It is no surprise considering the systematic methods which are fundamental to Zen meditation practice.

3. Counting the cycles of breathing

New research has shown that deep breathing has a positive impact on our bodies because it helps us cope with stress more skillfully. Most cutting-edge businesses have meditation rooms, and allow their staff to take a rest, relax and concentrate on breathing.

One method of meditation that is of particular benefit to those who find it difficult to focus on is counting the cycles of breathing. This method of meditation takes to focus a step further by giving a complex task to the meditator: count inhales, exhale, and one. Breathe in, exhale, two. Inhale, exhale, three, et cetera. Remaining completely conscious during this cycle is a strong attention exercise – many people find that their minds drifted until they could count to three. However, with time and persistence, their concentration capacity increases, and they can keep counting... The sky's the limit!

What about attention and meditation?

Sustained attention findings show that it can be done more effectively by people who practice guided meditation for concentrating on one specific task than by nonmeditators.

Especially when the assigned task was completely unexpected, they perform better, an indicator that preparedness and resilience improve with regular meditation.

- Selective caution. Meditators often have an advantage when it comes to focusing on the most important stimuli. Many who regularly train can restrict how much attention they pay to irrelevant sensory feedback and thus perform better in activities that require careful care.
- Commitment to Executive Regulation. This kind of focus reduces the propensity of the brain to actively process disruptive knowledge like thoughts about future or past events. Frequent meditators of mindfulness were found to perform especially well about executive function as opposed to non-meditators.

GUIDED CONCENTRATION MEDITATION

If you consider meditation difficult, then guided focus meditation may be a good option for you. Here is an instructor's voice that guides you through your meditation session. The session could be held at your home or in a group environment. Practicing guided meditation sometimes seems simpler than doing it alone. Still, it's important to stay alert because the very comfort of being guided and following directions is so relaxing that the mind starts to wander – or you're doing to doze off. As a meditator, the job is to note when that happens and to come back to the practice.

Meditation of focus should be practiced much of the time. You should teach yourself to stay in the moment and be mindful of thoughts coming and going. Keep aware of carrying out your everyday tasks. For example, as you eat, try to feel your food's texture and taste as you chew and consider the various sensations present in your body. The entire mouth is involved, salivary glands are activated, lots of muscles are involved in chewing and swallowing, and so on.

Don't do the rest! Don't listen to the radio, make a shopping list, check your emails, or read the papers. Just eat it, and feel you're enjoying it. To improve your concentration, use the act of eating or participating in other tasks while staying one-point concentrated on the task at hand.

After reading this book, it is apparent that you are interested in meditation practice and its results: making life more enjoyable and meaningful. And so we are! Mindworks is a non-profit organization whose mission is to share meaningful advice on meditation with you and with our followers around the world.

Chapter 5: HOW TO REVERSE NEGATIVE THINKING PATTERNS

Your emotions are primarily deciding the prism you perceive the world through. That purpose must explore the essence of your thoughts. Ultimately they are more positive than negative? Do they lay the foundations for a positive or negative approach?

Your genetics and climate are also helping to address those questions. The dichotomy of nature versus nutrition has been explored for centuries, but many believe the two are intricately interwoven. In other words, you are affected by both your genetic makeup and your natural environment.

The good news is that any of you need not feel threatened. You have a say on which thoughts you should be paying attention to. This may not always seem like that is the case because your thinking habits are becoming so normal, but you can substitute negative thoughts with more optimistic ones with a little insight and some time.

General Habits of Thinking

Patterns of negative thinking can cause needless tension and anxiety, paving the way for a gloomy outlook on life. Dr. David Burns describes common negative thinking habits, or cognitive illusions in his book, Feeling Good: The Modern Mood Therapy, such as:

- All-or-nothing Thinking: Thinking in black, white, or drastic words. You either behave as "great" or as "failure" in a way you name it.
- I can't remember I was eating a bag of potato chips. I skipped my food entirely. I am a complete and utter disappointment. Now I can just as well eat the whole pack.
- Overgeneralization: To assume inaccurately that one bad encounter would lead to a grim future filled with several more.
- I figured I did have the job. Then I'm never going to find one and are going to be unemployed forever.
- Magnification (or catastrophe): exaggerating negative incident specifics and overemphasizing your imperfections and worries, making events far larger than they are.

I fumbled at all those people for my vocabulary. They have to think I'm the dumbest person on the planet. My employer will probably blame me for this. And what am I going to do then?

- Emotional Reasoning: Assuming that the way you feel right is the truth of your reality.
- Lately, I've been feeling so nervous and stressed out, which must mean my issues are pretty major and almost difficult to solve.
- Must statements: Using "shall" phrases to reinforce action when they eventually leave you feeling irritated and under pressure.

After I eat pizza, I would work out.

I will send all those emails back to work.

For the remainder of the month, I will be eating super healthy.

Dr. Melanie Greenberg addresses two more specific forms of thought in an article in Psychology Today:

- Negative rumination: constant emphasis on negative consequences, leading to feelings of stuckness, anxiety, and even depression.
- You are overthinking: trying to anticipate and prepare for any imaginable situation, trying basically to control what's out of your control, trying to prevent pain or failure.

When can you break out of those negative habits of thinking and replace them with more positive thoughts? Here are five tips.

1. Practice mindfulness

To follow more optimistic forms of thought, you will first become aware of the existing ways of thinking. In practicing mindfulness, you will recognize and recognize the habits of thought that have become normal, then determine whether to pursue them or not. Mindfulness establishes a buffer between yourself and your emotions so that you can perceive yourself as distinct from them.

Incorporate focus into your morning or evening routine, sitting quietly for a couple of minutes (and slowly getting longer with practice). When a thought emerges, you simply turn the emphasis to your breath instead of binding yourself to it.

2. Answer your inner Criticism

Your inner critic likes to persuade you of facts that are obviously not true and sometimes make you feel pretty bad about yourself. Speak of the voice as a different entity from you. Challenge the lies which it is trying to tell you. Ask yourself: Is this valid? Is there evidence to support that assertion?

Another strategy is to thank the inner voice for their feedback, but then just say: No, thank you. I do not want to deal with such negative emotions. Or you could choose a shorter, more straightforward response like: Not now or Delete.

3. Know The Activators

Some individuals, events, and circumstances can put into motion a seemingly endless stream of negative thoughts (or maybe more than usual), so it's important to be conscious of it. Perhaps experiences with your boss or significant life decisions make you unnecessarily critical of yourself or doubt your self-worth. You will brace yourself and feel more in control of your emotions when you are aware of your causes, than slipping back into old negative thinking habits.

It's also helpful to recognize which cognitive biases you appear to replicate frequently, such as the ones listed above.

4. Write it Up

Putting emotions down on paper is not only a perfect way to unload your thoughts but also to understand more about their essence. Sometimes, you don't know how negative your emotions are. Negative habits of thought become repetitive over time, usually without even recognizing yourself. By writing them down, you can recognize the places you need your attention more easily.

Morning newspapering, first thing after you wake up, is the perfect time to place your stream of consciousness on paper.

5. Recite a Mantra

Reciting a mantra or positive reinforcement is a perfect way to drag yourself out and into the present moment from under the negative thoughts. This can be recited when you sense negativity spreading during the day or several times, to get into the habit of dwelling on them.

You can pick any word or sentence that will help bring you into the present and allow you to concentrate more on the positive. Here are some suggestions:

- I choose peace
- I am enough
- It is enough to do my best

6. Change your environment

Your thoughts can often sound so noisy that the only thing to do is to change the physical environment. Take a nature walk, go for a run, or meet a friend. The idea is to indulge in something other than the depressive loop so that when you are in a better headspace, you can come back to the problem later.

Pick an activity or location you find fun, and you know it will make you feel better. If you need someone else 's company, be sure to surround yourself with people who can encourage your positive thinking. (Steer off triggers!)

Negative thought habits can be hard to break, particularly after they have become repetitive. Patterns that have been in place for years are not going to be broken immediately, so being gentle and cooperative with yourself while you work through them is important.

Chapter 6: SLEEP IMPORTANT FOR MEMORY AND COGNITION

As noted in a recent digest of the week, sleep is important for well-being. Sleep deprivation risks include an increased chance of weight gain and the development of diseases such as common cold, heart disease, and diabetes, as well as more readily experienced attention, problem-solving, and decision-making impairments (1). Importantly, with only moderate sleep deprivation of 1-2 hours a night (that's around 6 hours of sleep), those risks increase.

Although you're hopefully persuaded that sleep is necessary for several reasons, our emphasis as learning scientists is on cognition and the ability to learn and remember, so I'll summarize one specific study showing the impact of sleep on learning for this blog posting.

Evidence of how sleep helps to learn

To investigate the impact of sleep on learning in the classroom, Scullin and colleagues gave a lecture on supply and demand to undergraduate students with no previous exposure to economics. Students were distributed to one of two classes at random. The first group watched the morning lecture and came back to take a test in the evening. The second group watched the evening lecture and came back to take a test in the morning. In this way, the time was kept constant from lecture to test, but only the second party slept between the lecture and the test.

The test was split into two pieces. Half of the questions were very similar to the types of questions that were used as examples during the lecture on supply and demand. The other half of the questions were called "integration" issues, which required students to integrate both supply and demand information to solve new complex problems.

The results showed that sleep group students performed about 8 percent better on the issues that were similar to those from the lecture. But students who had slept before taking the test performed 32 percent higher on the novel problems than those who had not slept! In other words, after sleeping, students retained more information, but their ability to understand and apply that information received the greatest benefit from sleep.

Why sleep aid learning?

One of the common misconceptions regarding sleep is that when nothing happens, it's simply a restful period, or in other words, the brain is still. On the opposite, the brain is very active while bed, even more so than during waking hours. Throughout the night, the brain goes through many different forms of sleep, often with very rapid movement and sometimes with what's called slow-wave sleep. (For more information on the various sleep stages, please visit helpguide.org.)

It is during slow-wave sleep that the brain begins to replay the information learned when awake, leading to memory consolidation – putting them into long-term storage (3). As the brain cycles during the night through the different phases of sleep, losing sleep means the recovery period is lost.

And, in the end ...

Students: Sleep is the best way to prepare for yourself. Having a good night's sleep can significantly help to retain information in class, appreciate the knowledge, and learn new information. In other words, if you get a good night's sleep every night (not just the night before the exam, though that night is also important), you're much more likely to do well on ANY test.

Parents: Get serious about sleeping. Bedtime is important at all stages of life, and the age of electronic devices and social media has made it harder to protect your child's health. Try to build healthy bedtime habits inside your kids. Hygiene tips for healthy sleep include:

- Try to sleep 7.5-9 hours a night. The number of hours needed varies from person to person, but for optimal operation, the vast majority of adults need about 7.5-9 hours anywhere.
- Only use the bed to lie in. If kids (or adults) associate the dormitory with work, socializing, or other "awake" activities, they are less likely to feel comfortable in that room.
- Do not take caffeine late in the day. Caffeine requires about 8 hours to get into your body. If your child (or you) is having dinner with a caffeinated drink, this will hinder the opportunity to fall asleep at night.
- Set and stick to a sleep schedule. Our bodies will use daytime to learn when to relax and get ready to sleep,

effectively setting up a circadian rhythm. Some evidence suggests a consistent sleep schedule could be even more critical to learning and memory than overall sleep time!

MEMORY AND SLEEP: HOW THEY WORK TOGETHER

Research published in Current Biology in July 2019 shows that a bad night's sleep — specifically, restless fast-eye movement (REM) sleep — negative effects on brain function, like amygdalae, work. These are almond-sized nuclei clusters situated deep within the temporal lobes of the brain and responsible for consolidating long-term learning memories, as well as collecting and storing memories associated with events that bring forth intense emotions such as sorrow, humiliation, fear, and anxiety.

Upon waking, study participants who endured disturbed REM sleep remained sensitive to previous-day emotional events. At the same time, well-rested individuals classified previous-day events as less emotional than they initially assumed, according to the researchers.

We have long been aware that mood, alertness, focus, and judgment are essential for a good night's sleep. Science has also established that sleep plays a crucial role in retaining memory. What we have not understood explicitly, at least until now, is how these cycles of sleep and memory are theoretically related and how they hurt how each affects the other.

Study authors written in Proceedings of the National Academy of Sciences in 2018 suggest that even a single night of sleep deprivation may cause beta-amyloid, a metabolic waste product, to accumulate in brain structures, including amygdalae, which regulate mood, emotion, memory, and learning ability and are involved in Alzheimer's disease development. The amygdalae maintain neural pathways to the hypothalamus, which regulates essential biological systems such as sleep, menstrual cycle, and circadian rhythm and interacts with the hippocampus, a key component in-memory processing.

Indeed, neural circuits linking the hippocampus to other brain regions are called repositories for storing episodic memories, specifically events, their position, and the emotions associated with them.

For memory to operate properly, there must be three essential processes:

- Acquisition: know something new, or experience something new
- Consolidation: incorporation of new knowledge into the brain, holding it together
- Remember: Access information after it has been stored

Acquisition and recollection occur while one is awake; acquisition, asleep; The brain responds to external stimuli while awake, and encodes new memories that are fragile at that stage and subject to forgetting. Through a substantially decreased sensitivity to external stimuli, the sleeping brain offers optimum conditions for consolidating information, which enhances and incorporates new memory into existing knowledge networks.

At one time, researchers believed sleep was shielding memory from outside stimuli from intrusion. Now we know that both REM and slow-wave sleep (SWS) are taking on more active roles in memory consolidation, processing different kinds of memories during different stages of sleep.

For example, a study in a 2018 issue of the Journal of Sleep Science shows that one night of lack of sleep can affect the working memory, which is vital for thinking and planning.

More worried though, study participants most affected by sleep deprivation, women, were unaware of their performance decline, raising their risk for accidents and errors. A prime example of such a risk is the relation between car crashes and sleep deprivation. Other studies suggest that the fact-based declarative memory mainly benefits from SWS-dominated sleep periods and procedural memory, remembering how to do something, is related to REM sleep.

While we still have much to know about sleep and memory as physicians and scientists, we can state with confidence that a good night's sleep improves focus on learning and understanding what we have learned. Here are a few tips for optimizing sleep quality and quantity:

- Daytime workout earlier – not several hours before bedtime.
- Reduce or avoid stimulants such as caffeine later in the day, and alcohol at night.
- Limit the naps to 30 minutes; after midday, do not snap.
- Stick to a sleep schedule; go to bed and wake up every day at around the same time, including weekends and holidays.

- Relax before bedtime, and clear your mind; read a book, listen to quiet music.
- Keep the evening cooler in the bedroom. I am using the "white noise" from a fan motor to cover annoying noises like that. Install shades that darken the room.
- Make sure you have a good mattress and consider sleeping on one pillow – not two or three.
- Don't eat a big meal or drink extra liquid just before bedtime.
- Stop using your computer, laptop, or smartphone right before bedtime. The screen light activates the brain and makes it difficult to fall asleep.

Sleep architecture is as important as quantity or quality. Proper bedtime and wake-up times allow us to go through the slow-wave and REM sleep phases. Alcohol, sedatives, and other medications can also reduce both slow-wave and REM sleep. And a cool bedroom, or hot bath before bed, enhances sleep enormously, slowly.

Chapter 7: MEMORY SCIENCE: TOP 10 PROVEN STRATEGIES TO REMEMBER MORE AND LEARN FASTER

I was still envious of people with unforgettable memories. You know, the kind of people who, with minimal effort, amass comprehensive information, while the rest of us fail to remember the name of the person we were introduced to seconds ago.

There is hope for us all, however. Much like we can strengthen every other muscle in our bodies, we can train our brains to remember more, and learn more quickly. You don't need to be born with a photographic memory (and almost no adults currently have a photographic memory, with a few notable exceptions obviously).

If you need to prepare for an exam, want to learn a foreign language, want to prevent awkward memory lapses (what is your manager's spouse's name again?), or just want to remain mentally healthy, it's easier to boost your memory than it seems. All it takes is to try out new memorization strategies or to make essential lifestyle changes. Below are 10 of the best tips and tricks to help improve your memory in short as well as the long term.

THE SCIENCE OF MEMORY

Next, let's think about how memory works, so we can appreciate the science behind specific strategies of memorization.

If memory – or how our brains make and remember memories – looks to you as mysterious, you're not alone. For at least 2,000 years, scientists and thinkers have been trying to find out how human memory functions – and are still making discoveries. For example, in 2016, British scientists won the world's largest neuroscience prize (1 million Euros) for their memory work – the discovery of a protein in the brain that plays a crucial role in memory formation and memory loss. There are still plenty of things to learn and to understand.

Nonetheless, we know that there are essentially three stages or phases for memory processing: encoding, storing, and recalling.

EnCoding

The first step towards creating a memory is called encoding: it's when you notice an event or find a piece of information, and your brain consciously perceives the sounds, images, physical feeling, or other sensory details involved.

Let's take your first trip to Las Vegas, for example. Your memory of that event is formed by your visual system (noticing, for instance, extravagantly designed buildings and lush landscaping), your auditory system (slot machine ringing), and maybe smell (the distinctive scents pumped into each casino).

"Evidence shows that we remember things better and maintain them longer when we use semantic encoding to attach meaning to them."

If you add all of these sensory inputs to the context or factual information, that's called semantic encoding. For example, if you connect the Bellagio Resort and Casino in Vegas with its location on a map or the fact that every 30 minutes the dancing fountain display takes place, you encode the Bellagio with semantic memory.

It is good to say, as evidence shows, that we remember words better and maintain them longer when we use semantic encoding to assign meaning to them.

Storage

All these little bits and pieces of information will then be processed in different parts of your brain. Your neurons (the nerve cells in your mind) are transmitting messages to each other about what you thought, essentially "talking" to each other and creating either temporary or long-lasting linkages. Neuroscientists say it's the neural activity, and the strength of those links makes a memory.

The neuronal network in our brains is the key to preserving and restoring memories

There are two types of memories: short- and long-term. Short-term or working memory is like a scratchpad in your brain. It is when the brain briefly retains information before either ignoring it or passing it to long-term memory — remembering, for example, what you want to order for lunch before calling the takeout. When your food is delivered and consumed, the data will be let go of your brain. Long-term memories are those memories that you hang on to for a couple of days or years — things like riding a bike or having your first dinner with the first person you fell in love with.

Both types of memories can weaken with age because, over time, the brain loses cells critical to those neuron-to-neuron connections – but that's not inevitable. You can exercise the brain as with muscle strength; with memory, it is "use it or lose it."

Recall

And eventually, the brain "replays" or revisits the nerve pathways produced when the memory was developed to get memory back. Recalling information over and over again helps to reinforce the associations and your memories, which is why methods such as updating your notes or using flashcards help you remember information.

But, if you recall anything, it's not an accurate reconstruction of the first time you've witnessed an occurrence or found a reality because your knowledge of the present situation is mixed with memory.

MEMORY AS EXPLAINED IN THE MIND OF MAN

Memories aren't frozen in time, so over time, new knowledge and ideas can be integrated into old memories. Remembrance can thus be considered an act of creative reimagination.

That's also why people may have false memories or can alter their memories of events over time.

So that we know some of how memory works, the knowledge can be used to strengthen our memory. We'll start with the improvements in lifestyle that we can make as they can boost more than just our memory, and then go through different memorization techniques.

Changes in lifestyle which can boost your memory

In general, improving your overall health with better sleep, daily exercise, and a better diet will improve your brain health — including memory — as well as your health. These three items should provide you with the best bang for your dollar to avoid memory loss and boost your overall memory.

1. Sleeping on It

Here's an easy way to boost your memory: after learning something new, get a good night's sleep, or take a power nap. One research study showed that people who slept for 8 hours after learning new faces and names could remember them better than those who didn't get the opportunity to sleep. And in reviewing two study datasets, psychologist Nicolas Dumay found that not only does sleep shield our brains form memories being lost, it also allows us to better remember memories.

What's that for? It seems our brains are being "reset" to sleep and are critical for memory and learning. If you're sleep-deprived, neurons in the brain are over-connected with so much electrical activity that you can't save fresh memories.

And this makes the case against cramming late-night for an exam or staying up all night to rehear the presentation. As demonstrated by The New York Times:

Do not sit up late refreshing Instagram at your usual time; hit the hay. Researchers have found the highest dose of so-called deep sleep in the first half of the night — the knocked-out-cold variety

— because this is when the brain consolidates facts and statistics and new words. This is territory for retention, and without it (if we stay up too late), we're foggier on those basic facts the next day.

Plan on naps, too! Researchers found that taking a snack of about 45-60 minutes right after learning something new could increase your memory by 500 percent.

So sleep thereon. If your boss or colleagues catch you at work napping, just show them those findings.

2. Get moving

Much as sleep is vital to your physical and mental well-being, so too is the other wellbeing pillar: exercise.

Our brains depend on oxygen to function correctly, so we need an adequate supply of oxygen-rich blood into our brains to get that oxygen. Just guess what? Exercise increases the circulation of blood into the brain. Studies at the National Institute on Ageing have found that physical activity, such as running, is related to enhanced memory. Exercise like this triggers high levels of a protein called cathepsin B, which travels into the brain to trigger neuronal growth and new hippocampal connections, an area in the brain that is thought to be critical to memory.

The experiments were carried out on rats, monkeys, and 43 sedentary university students who had to get fit for the research. Those subjects which have the most significant memory improvements? You know it: that following physical activity with the most considerable rise in cathepsin B.

Just don't rush to get your running shoes on, just yet. It could pay to wait after studying or learning something new. Exercising around 4 hours after learning could be better for memory recovery than exercising right afterward. Researchers are also unsure as to why delaying exercise is more successful than instantly working out, but maybe our brains need time to take up new knowledge before the brain-boosting workout.

3. Strengthen your diet

With all this advice, we don't want to sound like your mom or doctor, so here's the last suggestion focused on lifestyle: Eat healthily.

Perhaps you know it, but saturated and trans fats – the kind you get from red meat and butter – are correlated with impaired memory. Just like cholesterol can expand in the arteries of your heart, so it can build up in your brain. Harvard Health describes:

The accumulation of cholesterol plaques in brain blood vessels can damage brain tissue, either by small blockages causing silent strokes or a more significant, more severe stroke. Be that as it may, brain cells are deprived of the oxygen-rich blood they need to function correctly, which may impair memory and think.

Diets such as the Mediterranean diet, consisting primarily of vegetables and berries, olive oil, fish, and nuts — rich in healthy unsaturated fats — have been related in various studies to memory improvements and lower memory loss levels.

Is the brain ready to feed? Here's the Mayo Clinic's guide to getting the Mediterranean diet started.

Mnemonics Help You Remember More

Besides leading a balanced lifestyle, there are unique memory strategies that can allow you to better recall specifics of everything you know. "Mnemonics" refers to any system or device designed to help memory – usually letter patterns, ideas, or associations, such as ROYGBIV to remember the rainbow's colors.

Here are some of the most familiar and most popular mnemonics:

4. Try Common Mnemonics

The most common mnemonics help you recall words or sentences quickly. For example, to remember the order of planets orbiting the earth, you might have learned "My Very Educated Mother Just Served Us Nine Pizzas" in grade school (where the first letter of each word stands for Mercury, Venus, Earth, Mars, Jupiter, Saturn, Uranus, Neptune, and Pluto, respectively).

Here are a few more examples:

- Acronyms or Mnemonics expression: Similar to the planetary example above, thinking "Every Good Boy Does Fine" can help you remember the lines of the music Treble Clef (EGBDF).
- Music mnemonics: Music is a strong mnemonic as it offers an information structure and promotes repetition. Recalling a catchy song is a lot better than identifying a long series of words or letters, like your password for your bank account. (It's also why advertisers sometimes use jingles to put their ads in your brain. Don't get me started with that Kars4Kids jingle.) You've already learned the alphabet from the ABC song, so if you're researching a common subject, there's a chance there's a song for that, like learning the 50 states in the U.S. with the Fifty Fun U.S. song or learning all the elements from the regular t.

- Rhyming Mnemonics: maybe you remember the rhyme that begins with
"January, March, June, and November 30 days?" Rhymes are similar to

  mnemonics in music. Once each line rhymes to the end, it produces a song-like rhythm that is easy to recall. One phrase I heard from watching a cooking show: "Looks the same, cooks the same"—a reminder that even cooking ingredients should be diced and dice uniformly.
- Rhyming Peg System: Memorize a list of things using the "peg system" (also known as the "hook system") using number rhymes. In this scheme, you memorize a picture of a word with which you rhyme for each number. That image provides the things you want to remember, especially in order, with a "hook" or "peg."

So let's say you had a list of things to purchase in the grocery store, for example, milk, cookies, bananas, and bacon. You'd use the peg device to:

1. First, know the rhyming board, or build it. A = bun. 2 = zoo. Three = árbol. Quatre = Window. And so on.
2. Form a vivid mental image for every number of rhyming objects. (What looks like the bread bun? What kind of shoe is that? What color are the leaves on the tree? What kind of hardware does the door have?)
3. Picture the Rhyming object with your list item for each item on your shopping list. For example, if "milk," "one," = "bun" is the first thing on your list, then imagine a container of milk being squeezed between a giant bread bun. We see a package of cookies dropping into the zoo's lion's enclosure, a maple tree inside the store with bananas

hanging off a branch, and slices of bacon stuck in a black door's mailbox window.

Memorizing a list this way involves some effort and imagination, but you'll maintain the knowledge much longer than if you're only trying to memorize the words in order. And once you have the foundation rhyming peg down, this can be reused for any potential lists.

5. Build a Palace of Memories

"The number one technique we top memory athletes use is still and will always be the memory palace. It should be that if someone were to learn one thing. "- Nelson Dellis, four-time US memory champion

A memory palace is a mnemonic tool that is as tried-and-true as it gets — and that deserves its portion. The memory palace (or mental palace or "loci method") technique, invented by orators in ancient Roman and Greek times, is both successful and fun to use, whether you're trying to recall a speech you've got to deliver, specifics of a case you're working on (a la Sherlock Holmes), or your grocery list. Indeed, four-time U.S. Memory Champion Nelson Dellis — who claims to have an average memory — says, "The number one strategy that we top memory athletes use is still and will still be the memory palace.

In the technique of memory palace, you connect a place that you are familiar with — such as your apartment, the block on which you grew up, or the path you take to work or school — with the things you want to recall. This works because you are visually pegging (or "placing") versions of what you want to remember in locations you already have clear memories of.

To use the Palace memory technique:

1. Imagine standing in your memory palace. Even if it's not a palace, your home is a great one to start with.
2. Walkthrough this palace, mentally noticing distinctive features that you can use to store things you want to remember. Each stop along that path is a "loci" to which you can add the idea or the object. For, e.g., your front door may be one locus, your foyer's table second loci, your living room's lamp another. Commit those features to memory, so the path and items in it will be imprinted in your mind when you think of your house.
3. Associate the loci in your palace with what you need to recall. For example, if you had a list of groceries at the front door, you could imagine milk pouring from the inside over the door, like a waterfall of milk when you get to the foyer and the table buckles down to the ceiling under the weight of all the chocolate chip cookies piled on it. And you see neon yellow bananas instead of a light-bulb in your living room window.

It sounds pretty absurd, but as we will discuss later in more detail, the better you can make your memories, the more visual, animated, and outrageous.

6. Thinking Chunking Further

Chunking is another mnemonic tool that can memorize vast quantities of information. You will still use this. To recall or share a phone number, you're likely to chunk the numbers, so they're easier to remember: "888" "555" "0000" instead of the more memory-intensive "8 8 8 5 5 0 0 0 0." Evidence shows that, on average, the human brain can keep four different items in its (short-term) memory functioning. Yet by sorting information into smaller sets, we can, as The Atlantic puts it, "hack the boundaries of our working memory" to recall more.

The technique of chunking involves grouping objects, identifying patterns within them, and organizing the objects. For example, you might group items on your grocery list by lane, or search for connections between incidents in a historical context to build chunks of them, such as moments in the 1920s that involved the US Constitution.

Chunking works because our brains are well trained to search for patterns and attach. Picking Brain explains:

Our memory system is much more powerful, reliable, and intelligent than it could ever be to extract useful structure from raw data without such sophisticated methods [as chunking].

To put this into action yourself, you may group vocabulary words for a new language you are learning by subject, arrange items in a list by the first letter or by the number of letters they have, or link items with the larger whole they might be involved in (e.g., apples, brown sugar, pie crust, butter = apple pie).

Everyday Strategies for Memorizing

Besides memory aids or methods like the ones above, there are also wider tactics that can help you better recall what you experience every day — techniques that work regardless of what you seek to memorize.

7. Make New Relations That Is Visual (and Maybe Odd)

Glass shattered. Stinky sauces. Screaming out, infants swaddled. As Dellis gave me a training course on memorization strategies in preparation for the 2012 U.S. Memory Championship, the one aspect that stuck out to me among all the approaches he discussed was how vivid – and sometimes nonsensical – the memories you are making the need to be fixed among memory.

Visualization is the main memory capacity. It's hard to recall names and numbers because they're abstract, and our minds can't quickly hold on them. But our brains have much easier storing and recalling images.

Here are some visual tricks which are working well:

Turn the names sound into images: As soon as a stranger says, "Hi, I'm Mike," and you say, "Hey Mike" – poof! You forget the name of this guy because you didn't connect that word with anything about that guy (maybe it was stored in your short-term memory, but probably not). You need to have something more related to "Mike."

The best approach is to transform the abstract into a sound and visual representation with the technique of memory palace and other memorization strategies that deal with symbols (such as letters and numbers)—using the sounds within the word to make it a picture. In the "Mike" case, you could think of a microphone picture. Build a picture for each syllable, for multi-syllable names. For "Melanie," you might think of crushing it with melon and a knee.

The second step then is to peg (or anchor) the picture to the position you'll know. When your new friend, Mike, has exceptionally big eyes, you might picture microphones bouncing out of every sight of his.

It is similar to the technique of memory palace. Still, instead of anchoring new visual information to a location, you are arriving it to a physical feature of whatever you try to remember.

Animate the images: The better you can make these images, the more animated and vivid. Doing so creates healthier, novel connections between that word or number and an image in your brain.

Engage as many of your senses as possible: Recall how your feelings initiate the encoding process with the brain? When you tap your sense of hearing, taste, and smell, you'll remember abstract things like names and numbers better. Maybe you'll hear audio feedback from the microphones on the Mike example. Maybe some of the fruit gushes out of the melon in the Melanie example, and you can smell it.

Similar techniques apply when it comes to numbering. You can associate numbers 0-9 to images, which will help you remember long numbers strings better. 0, could be a doughnut, for example; 1 could be a flagpole; 2 could be a swan. Then imagine a swan swimming past a flagpole to pick at a doughnut, to recall the number 210. (Memory champions like Dellis encode double- or triple-digit numbers with photos so they can memorize hundreds of digits in five minutes, 00 equals Ozzy Osbourne, 07 is James Bond, for example).

8. Write them down, don't type them out

Place your laptop away. You're more likely to remember handwritten notes than those you type.

There are a few reasons why when it comes to memory, handwriting is preferable to using your laptop. First, the physical act of writing, called the reticular activating system (RAS), activates cells at the base of your brain. Once the RAS is activated, the brain is paying more attention to what you are doing. Similar to typing on a keyboard where similar keys represent each letter, the brain becomes more involved in forming each letter while you are writing by hand.

Research has also shown that people prefer to transcribe lectures verbatim while taking notes on their laptops. Conversely, we prefer to reframe the knowledge in our terms while making notes by hand – a more involved kind of learning.

Maybe even better: Create mind maps for subjects you're learning. It combines the visual element with handwritten words – remember, our brains latch onto images.

9. Using Spaced Repetition

You know how to prep for a test or learn something new, like some fascinating facts from a book, and then forget what you learned immediately? Unless we're always trying to maintain the detail, we're likely to lose it – in days or weeks. This is the natural exponential essence of forgetting, as the forgetting curve depicts:

When you want to know something for the long term, such as vocabulary in a foreign language or information you need for your career, repetition spaced is the most effective way of learning the subject. As Gabriel Wyner states in his excellent book on language learning, Fluent Forever: "A Spaced Repetition System (SRS) at its most simple level is a to-do list that adjusts according to your results."

You'll start with short intervals between practice sessions (two to four days). Each time you recall correctly, you can raise the period (e.g., nine days, three weeks, two months, six months, etc.) and easily exceed intervals of years.

That makes the sessions hard enough to push information into long-term memory continuously. If you forget a word, you're going to start with short intervals again and work your way back to long ones until the word sticks. This pattern keeps you focused on your weaker memories while your best memories are retained and deepened. Since well-remembered terms inevitably disappear into the far future, the daily practice provides a balance between old and new.

The way to avoid forgetting is to use a spaced scheme of repetition, with your physical flashcards or an app like the Anki or Pauker. Digital devices are more convenient, of course, but a powerful learning experience is a process of making your cards – including discovering photos to connect to what you're doing. Regular reviews are best for both approaches, but any form of daily routine can help you learn more quickly and remember.

10. Share What You Know

Eventually, there's the adage that "the best way to know anything is to show it to anyone else." Once I asked the Zapier team what their favorite form of memorizing and learning was, most people spoke about teaching, explaining, or just suggesting to anyone else what they've learned.

As [students] prepare to teach, they organize their knowledge, improving and recalling their understanding. And when they describe the knowledge to [a computerized character learning from Betty's Brain] students, they find knots and holes in their thought.

A 2009 Betty's Brain research published in the Journal of Science Education and Technology showed that students who were interested in teaching her spent more time studying and understanding the content more thoroughly.

Bonus Tip: Offload the Memory You Don't Want

The human brain is amazing. Since our neurons can store a lot of memories at a time, our mental storage capacity is somewhere in the range of 2.5 petabytes (million gigabytes) – enough to carry nonstop TV shows worth 300 years.

That said, while we are not running the risk of our brains being complete, there is plenty of information that we come across that we can import through our digital devices. Memorizing information requires a lot of time, so we can concentrate on the details we need to commit to memory.

Evernote will stand up for your second brain to help you recall something or use one of the several other note-taking programs to do the same.

The memory may still be a mystery to us, but studies have shown that the above strategies help you remember more of what you're studying. I don't have a photographic memory and still fail to remember where I left my keys, but when I try to use at least one of the above strategies to commit it to memory, it seems to stick in my brain. At least, I had fewer moments of "what's your name again?"

Chapter 8: LEARNING FASTER AND RECALL MORE 20 TIPS & TRICKS

The following are only a few learning ideas about how to make the brain smarter and faster.

1. Learn New Stuff:

Newer things learning always keeps the brain busy. It makes the brain get out of the comfort zone, and the wire itself to learn some new ways. It is a fact that when a person begins walking or begins to learn the language like Java, the brain initially struggles to understand but gradually adapts the entire process. From a new language to a more recent skill or subject, art form, or sports, one can learn anything new, something that the brain was not used to before.

2. Play the puzzles and the mind games:

Solving puzzles puts the brain in thought mode. The more it seeks to find the problem answers or the quiz, the more it opens up to new ideas. Seek to solve various puzzles from Sudoku to the crossword or several other mental games that are available these days that will help you learn things faster.

Brain games are similar to physical exercise where one pushes the physical limit to reinforce one's muscle, and likewise, brain nerves need to develop beyond their convenient zone. This brain training will enhance the brain's ability to learn fast.

3.   Eat well:

Food to the mind and the body is like fire. Make sure you eat food on time, and don't let hunger starve you. It is a common phenomenon when you are hungry and have difficulty remembering or thinking anything. Also, make sure to eat correctly, avoid regular alcohol, or the food is too heavy to digest. Evite heavy afternoon feeding as it reduces brain capacity to function effectively. Know what's best for you to eat and prepare a diet chart so you'll learn more efficiently and remember more.

4.   Sleep well:

Numerous researchers have proven over the years that a decent 7-8 hour sleep is safe for the brain to function effectively. The lack of sleep impairs brain health, and the brain will not be able to function correctly and will have difficulty recalling anything.

Only by adequately sleeping, one can see the difference in how it performs well and recalls well. Most people prefer to sleep less with too much tension in life and pay attention to the sleeping schedule.

Seek early sleep, and wake up early in the morning. Make dinner at least two hours before you go to bed, stop using cell phones until you go to sleep. A healthy and sound sleep is secret to a faster brain and more things to remember.

5.   Good meditation:

With so much tension going on in both our professional and personal lives. Even sleep is not enough to calm the mind at times.

It is usually a daunting task for us to learn a foreign language because most of us are used to our mother tounges. But researchers have shown that people who can understand more than two languages have the greater brain capacity to learn and function better.

Learning a new language is, therefore, quite a time-consuming process, and makes the brain go out of the comfort zone in the primary communication source. Once it is achieved, then it is never difficult to learn anything new.

19.   Build a mental chamber:

As can be seen in various detective shows, where the detectives have a mental room where they keep secure all their thoughts. This is a fascinating and highly successful way of doing stuff. Close your eyes and build a space of mind in your head, give it the color, look, and feel in space.

Whenever you need to recall something of significant significance, try putting any crucial detail in there. If you feel the right thing you can't remember, just close your eyes and see yourself in the same mental room. At first, it may seem impossible, but when your brain thinks and learns ten times faster, it works the best.

20.   Keep asking:

Children usually have clear minds and appear to lose their brain memory capacity as one develops. One such interesting point to remember here is that children are naturally curious and continue to question everything they see around them and save a portion of your child inside you, and continue to question things around you, be curious and enthusiastic about everything.

Seek to find the answers to those questions and explore it more closely as a child does. The secret to the great memory and increased brainpower is to keep your childhood part of yourself. This will make your brain quicker to learn skills than regular times.

Concluding:

In our everyday lives, the human brain is like any other machine. Because we are constantly operating the system in our environment, cooling the brain also always needs the treatment for it. Should not get into circumstances that make you unhappy or cause discomfort because the emotional fluctuation affects the capacity of the mind to function. You will improve your brain to function quicker and easier by following these points on how to train your brain to remember.

Chapter 9: HOW TO LEARN SMART: 20 WAYS TO LEARN FASTER

That's about how many hours a week there are.

If you're a student, you probably don't feel this is enough. I know ... You've got so many tasks to do, projects to work on, and tests to study for. Plus, you've got other activities and obligations. And even you want a social life.

Wouldn't it be great if you were able to study more intelligently (not harder), get good grades, and lead a happier life? It would, of course. This is why I have written this book.

The primary aim of education is not to get straight A's. Yet learning how to read is a critical competency in life. So, I spent hours scouring scientific papers and academic journals to find the best ways to know more.

I am a pure lifelong student myself, and I have completed my formal education ever since. I've used almost all of the tips presented in this book throughout my academic career, so I can check that they work.

Let's the kick-off. Here are 20 ways to learn faster in the sciences.

1. Learn the same knowledge in different ways.

The study shows that various stimuli activate different parts of the brain (Willis, J. 2008). The more regions of the brain that are activated, the more likely you can perceive the information and retain it.

So you could do the following for learning a specific topic:

- Read the class notes
- Read the textbook
- Look up other tools online
- Make a Mind Map
- Show someone what you have learned
- Do problems in practice from a variety of sources

You can't do all of these things in one sitting, of course. But every time you revisit the subject, use a different tool or process-this way, you can learn faster.

2. Study several subjects each day, instead of only concentrating on one or two topics.

Studying several subjects every day to help you stay focused is more successful than digging deeply into one or two subjects (Rohrer, D. 2012).

For instance, if you're studying for math, history, physics, and chemistry exams, it's best to learn a bit about each subject each day. This approach will help you learn faster than just Monday's math, Tuesday's history, Wednesday's physics, Thursday's chemistry, and so on.

Why? For what?

Because if you study a lot of the same subject in a single day, you are likely to confuse similar information.

So as a tip for quicker learning, spread your study time for each subject. Doing so will give your brain more time to consolidate your learning.

3. Check the details frequently, rather than cramming it.

If you want to move the information from your short-term memory to your long-term memory, periodic review is essential. This will help you receive better grades for your tests.

As the research (Cepeda, N. 2008) shows, periodic review beats hand-down cramming.

The optimum analysis time varies according to how long you want the information to be kept. But experience – on my own and from working with students – informs me that the following evaluation cycles work well (I describe the whole periodic review system in this book):

- 1st assessment: 1 day after new information has been learned
- 2nd assessment: 3 days from the first review
- 3rd assessment: 7 days following 2nd assessment
- 4th assessment: 21 days after revision 3
- 5th assessment: 30 days after 4th assessment
- 6th assessment: 45 days after the fifth review • 7th assessment: 60 days after the sixth review

4. Sit at the class front.

If you decide where to sit during class, grab a front seat. Studies show that students sitting at the front continue to get higher scores for the test (Rennels & Chaudhari, 1988). The average student scores are as follows, depending on where they sat in class

(Giles, 1982):

- Its front rows: 80%

- Intermediate rows: 71.6 percent
- Rows back: 68.1 percent

Such results were obtained under conditions where teacher-assigned seating positions were assigned. This means that it is not only a case of the more motivated students choosing to sit at the front, and the less motivated students choosing to sit behind.

You'll be able to see the board by sitting at the front and hear the teacher more clearly, and your concentration will also improve.

Now you know where the class seats are best!

5. Don't indulge in multitasking.

The research is conclusive: multitasking makes you less successful, more distracted, and more stupid. Studies also show that people who claim to be good at multitasking are not better at multitasking than the average.

Efficient students only focus on one thing at a time. So don't try to study while also responding to text messages intermittently, watching TV, and checking your Twitter feed.

Here are some tips for improving your concentration:

- Turn off phone notifications
- Detach your phone, or turn it to airplane mode
- Logout from all instant messaging services
- Turn off access to the Internet on your computer
- Using the Freedom app

- Close all windows of your internet browser that are not related to the task you are working on
- Remove clutter from your field of research

6. The information is condensed, summarized, and compressed.

Use mnemonic devices such as acronyms, as these have been shown to increase learning efficiency.

E.g., # 1

If you wish to memorize the electromagnetic spectrum to increase the frequency, this acronym/sentence could be used:

Raging Martians Use X-ray guns to invade Venus

(The electromagnetic spectrum to increase the frequency is: Radio, Microwave, Infrared,
Visible, Ultraviolet, X-rays, Gamma rays.)

Case # 2

Question: Stalactites and stalagmites-who grow from the top of the cave and who grows from the ground?

Answer: Stalactites are growing from above, while stalagmites are growing from the ground up.

Research smart wherever possible, use mnemonic tools. You can also summarize the information into a comparison table, diagram, or mind map. These tools will help you to learn the information much more quickly.

7. Take notes manually, rather than using your laptop.

Scientists support this, and not only because when using your phone, but you are also more likely to give in to online distractions. Even when only note-taking laptops are used, learning is less effective (Mueller, P. 2013).

Why? For what?

Since students making notes by hand prefer to interpret the information and reframe it.

By contrast, laptop note-takers tend to write down what word-for-word is said by the teacher, without first processing the information.

Students who take notes by hand, therefore, do best in exams and examinations.

8. Write the worries down.

Am I going to do well on this exam?

What if I forget about essential concepts and equations?

What if the examination is more demanding than expected?

Possibly, these kinds of thoughts run through your mind before you take an exam. But if those thoughts run wild, the anxiety that accompanies them may affect your grades.

Here's the answer ...

Researchers at the University of Chicago have discovered in one experiment that students who wrote about their feelings about a 10-minute upcoming exam performed better than students who did not. The researchers say this technique is particularly useful for ordinary worriers.

Psychologist Kitty Klein has also shown that expressive writing improves memory and learning in the form of journaling. Klein argues that such writing allows students to convey their negative feelings, thereby allowing them to be less disturbed by those feelings.

To be less anxious, take 10 minutes to write down all the things you're worried about regarding the upcoming exam. You'll get better grades as a result of that simple exercise.

9. Test yourself often.

Decades of study have shown that self-testing is essential if the academic performance is to be improved.

In one experiment, psychologist Keith Lyle from the University of Louisville taught two groups of undergraduates the same course on statistics.

At the end of each lecture, Lyle asked the students for the first group to complete a four- to the six-question quiz. The quiz was based on the content that he had studied.

Lyle hasn't given the students any quizzes for the second group.

At the end of the course, Lyle discovered that the first group outperformed the second significantly on all four midterm examinations.

So don't just read your textbook or lesson notes passively. Study smart by challenging the main concepts and the equations. And as you prepare for a test, do as many practice questions from different sources as you can.

10. Connect what you are learning to something you know

already.

The scientist's Henry Roediger III and Mark A. McDaniel demonstrate in their book, Make It Stick: The Science of Good Learning, that the more intensely you link new concepts to concepts you already understand, the quicker you learn the latest information.

If you are thinking about electricity, for example, you might connect it to the water flow. Voltage is similar to water pressure; the water flow rate is equal to current, a battery is identical to a pump, and so forth.

Another example: White blood cells can be thought of as "soldiers" defending our body against diseases, which are the "enemies."

It takes time and effort to think about how to link new information to what you already know, but it's worth the investment.

11. Readout loud, essential information.

Studies have been carried out, which show that reading loud information helps students learn faster than reading silently.

Which is the reason for that?

You both see and hear this when you read the information out loud. On the other side, you just see it when you're processing knowledge silently.

Reading every single phrase of an available collection of notes out loud isn't realistic. This would take far too long.

So here's the method that I would recommend:

Step 1: Express the fundamental concepts/equations as you read your notes. Don't avoid memorizing certain main concepts/equations; stress them and push forward.

Step 2: After completing Step 1 for the entire set of notes, go back to the underlined parts, and read as many times as you deem necessary each critical concept/equation out loud. Slowly read out every concept/equation.

Step 3: Take a three-minute break after you've done this for each of the main concepts/equations highlighted.

Step 4: When your three-minute break is over, go one at a time to each underscored concept/equation and cover it (either with your hand or with a piece of paper). Test yourself to see if you did memorize it.

Step 5: Repeat Steps 2, 3, and 4 for the concepts/equations you did not memorize successfully.

12. Take breaks from research regularly.

Taking daily breaks of research increases overall efficiency and concentration (Ariga & Lleras, 2011).

That's why it's not a smart idea to just hole up in your room to prepare for an exam for six hours straight. You may feel like you've done a lot this way, but the research shows otherwise. And for every 40 minutes of work, take a 5- to 10-minute break.

I suggest using a timer or a stopwatch to remind you when to take a break, and when to return to analysis.

Refrain from using your phone or computer during your break, as these devices prevent you from fully relaxing your mind.

13. At the end of each study, session, reward yourself.

Set a clear incentive for completing the session before commencing a study session. In doing so, you will be promoting memory formation and learning (Adcock RA, 2006).

The payment could be as simple as:

- Go for a short hike
- Eat a balanced snack
- Listen to your favorite music
- stretch
- Do a couple of practice sets
- To play musical instruments
- Take a shower

At the end of each session, reward yourself-you will study smarter and learn faster.

14. Concentrate on the process and not the result.

Students who are successful at school focus on learning the information, not on trying to get a particular grade.

Work by Stanford psychologist Carol Dweck indicates that these students ...

- Focus on commitment and not the end product
- Focus on process, not accomplishment
- Assume that, even in their poor subjects, they will improve as long as they put in the time and hard work
- Coping with challenges
- Defines success as challenging yourself to learn something different, not straight A's

Not-so-successful students tend to set targets for results, while good students tend to set targets for learning.

What is the difference between the two styles of goals?

The goals of success (e.g., having 90 percent on the next math exam, having into a topranked school) are to look smart and prove to others.

By contrast, learning goals (e.g., every other day doing three algebra problems, learning five new French words a day) are about mastery and growth.

Most schools stress the importance of obtaining a certain examination score or passing a certain number of subjects. Ironically, if you want to meet – and exceed – those standards, it would be better to ignore the desired outcome and instead concentrate on the learning process.

15. Drink a minimum of eight glasses of water a day.

You probably think you're drinking enough water, but studies show that up to 75 % of people are in a chronic dehydration condition.

Dehydration is bad for your brain – and so are your examination grades.

Researchers at the University of East London have found that the total intellectual processing capacity of the brain diminishes when you are dehydrated (Edmonds, C. 2013). Additional research has shown that dehydration shrinks even the grey matter in your brain.

The fast way out?

Drink a total of eight glasses of water a day. Carry a bottle of water everywhere you go and drink water until you start feeling thirsty.

And if you do an exam, bring a bottle of water with you. Drink some water every 40 minutes or so. That will help you stay hydrated and improve the performance of your exam. Plus, this also serves as a brief break for refreshing your mind.

16. Exercise 3 times a week, at least.

Exercising is good for the body. It is good for your brain, too.

Different studies showed that exercise ...

- Makes your memory better
- Boost brain function
- Decreases incidence of depression
- Helps avoid diseases such as diabetes, cancer, and osteoporosis
- Makes your night easier
- Cut down on work
- Getting your mood better

Exercising is a wonder treatment!

So to study smarter, work out for 30 to 45 minutes each time at least three times a week. You're going to be healthier and more energetic, and you're going to remember better information, too.

17. Sleep a night for at least eight hours, and do not pull all-nights.

So far, I have talked to 20,000 students and worked with them. Not a single one has told me he or she gets eight hours of sleep a night consistently.

"It's just too much to do," I hear the students say, repeatedly. As a student, sleep sometimes seems more like a requirement than a privilege.

But what should the research say about sleep?

The research shows that if you get enough sleep, you'll be more focused, learn faster, and improve your memory. You'll also be more effective in dealing with stress.

This is a fine grade recipe.

So, at least eight hours of sleep a night. This will make your study sessions more productive, and you won't have to spend as much time hitting the books as possible.

Additionally, sleep expert Dan Taylor says that learning the most challenging material right before going to bed makes it easier to remember the next day. So, whenever possible, arrange your schedule so that you can study the most challenging subject right before you go to sleep.

And last but not least, don't pull all-nights. As work by psychologist Pamela Thacher reveals, students pulling all-nights get lower grades and make more reckless mistakes.

18. Eat those blueberries.

Blueberries are rich in flavonoids which reinforce connections within the brain and stimulate brain cell regeneration.

Researchers at Reading University find eating blueberries enhances both short and long-term memory (Whyte, A. &

Williams, C. 2014). Blueberries could also help prevent degenerative diseases such as Alzheimer's disease.

19. Eat the chicken and eggs.

A team of Boston University researchers conducted a 10-year long term study of 1,400 adults. They found participants who had high choline diets performed better on memory testing.

Choline is the precursor to acetylcholine, vital to the formation of new memories.

What Foods are Choline Heavy?

Chicken and eggs (the yolk of the egg contains 90 percent of the total egg choline).

You should breathe a sigh of relief just in case you are concerned about the high cholesterol content of egg yolks. Recent studies show that eggs are healthy food for just about everyone, including the yolk.

And if you are a vegetarian there are alternatives in your diet to get choline:

- Lentils
- Sunflower seeds
- Pumpkin seeds
- Almonds
- Cabbage
- Cauliflower
- Broccoli

20. Eat fatty acids made with omega-3.

Omega-3 fatty acids are essential to function in the brain. One experiment (Yehuda, S. 2005) also showed that taking a mixture of omega-3 and omega-6 fatty acids decreased anxiety in the student test and increased concentration in mind.

Omega-3 fatty acids are associated with the prevention of high blood pressure, heart disease, diabetes, arthritis, osteoporosis, depression, ADHD, dementia, Alzheimer's, asthma, colorectal cancer, and prostate cancer.

That is a superb selection!

Here are omega-3 fatty acid-rich foods:

- Salmon
- Sardines
- Mackerel
- Trout
- Flaxseed
- Pumpkin seeds
- Walnuts

The ending line is

This book, with a lot of information. But don't feel frustrated, because, at one shot, there is no need to enforce anything.

As the proverb goes ...

How about swallowing an elephant? One morsel at a time.

Similarly, do it one tip at a time to implement all 20 recommendations in this book. Focus on a single information a week, or even an end a month.

Once you have turned the tip into a daily habit of learning, proceed to the next.

Don't allow the aim of having straight A's to become an unhealthy obsession in the process. Education is more about getting good grades, after all.

This is about pursuing excellence. It's about having your strengths cultivated. And it is about learning and developing so that you can make a more productive contribution.

It requires hard work, but I know that you are up to the challenge.

Chapter 10: 14 NORMAL WAYS TO IMPROVE YOUR MEMORY

From time to time, everyone has moments of forgetfulness, particularly when life gets busy.

While this can be a perfectly natural phenomenon, it can be frustrating to have a bad memory.

Genetics plays a role in the loss of memory, particularly in neurological severe conditions such as Alzheimer's disease. Research has also shown that diet and lifestyle can have a significant effect on memory.

Here are 14 evidential ways to naturally improve your memory.

1. Eat Less Sugar

Overeating added sugar was associated with many health conditions and chronic illnesses, including cognitive decline.

Research has shown that a diet loaded with sugar can contribute to poor memory and decreased brainpower, particularly in the brain region where short-term memory is stored.

One study of more than 4,000 people, for example, found that those with a higher intake of sugary beverages such as soda had lower overall brain volumes and more imperfect memories on average compared to those who consumed less sugar.

Not only does cutting back on sugar help your memory, but it also improves your overall health.

Research has shown that people who eat tons of added sugar daily may have weaker memory and lower brain volumes than those who eat less.

2. Try a fish oil supplement

Fish oil is high in eicosapentaenoic acide (EPA) and docosahexaenoic acid (DHA) omega-3 fatty acids.

These fats are essential for overall health, reducing the risk of heart disease, reducing inflammation, alleviating stress and anxiety, and slowing mental decline.

Many studies have shown that the consumption of fish and fish oil supplements can improve memory, particularly in the elderly.

One analysis of 36 older adults with moderate cognitive impairment showed that shortterm and working memory scores substantially improved after 12 months of taking concentrated fish oil supplements.

A recent review showed that when adults with mild memory loss symptoms took DHA- and EPA-rich supplements, such as fish oil, they experienced improved episodic memory.

Both DHA and EPA are vital to the brain's health and function and also help reduce inflammation in the body that has been associated with cognitive decline.

The omega-3 fatty acids EPA and DHA are rich in Fish and fish oil supplements. Consuming them can help improve short-term, working, and episodic memory, particularly in the elderly.

3. Make Time to Meditate

The practice of meditation can, in many ways, have a positive effect on your health.

It is calming and stimulating, reducing tension and pain, decreasing blood pressure, and even improving memory.

In reality, it has been shown that meditation raises grey matter in the brain. Grey matter contains cell bodies in the neurons.

Grey matter declines as you age, which hurts memory and cognition.

Meditation and calming methods have been shown to enhance short-term memory in people of all ages, from people in their 20s to elderly people.

For example, one study found that college students from Taiwan who engaged in meditation activities such as mindfulness had significantly better spatial working memory than students who did not practice meditation.

Spatial working memory is the capacity to retain knowledge about object locations in space and interpret it in your mind.

Meditation is not only good for your body, but it is also good for your brain, too. Research suggests that meditation will increase grey matter in the brain and enhance the working spatial memory. 4. Keep Healthy Weight

Maintaining healthy body weight is vital to the well-being and is one of the best ways to keep your body and mind in perfect condition.

Various studies have identified obesity as a risk factor for cognitive decline.

Ironically, being obese can cause changes in memory-associated genes in the brain, influencing memory negatively.

Obesity can also contribute to insulin resistance and inflammation, which can have a detrimental effect on the brain.

A survey of 50 people aged between 18 and 35 showed that a higher body mass index was associated with substantially more inadequate memory test output.

Obesity is also linked to an increased risk of developing Alzheimer's disease, a progressive disease that destroys memory and cognitive function.

Obesity is a cognitive risk factor. Maintaining an index of body mass within the normal range will help you prevent several issues linked to obesity, including impaired memory.

5. Get Sleep Enough

Lack of proper sleep has long been linked to poor memory.

Sleep plays an essential role in memory consolidation, a process that reinforces shortterm memories and transforms them into long-lasting memories.

Research suggests you could be adversely affecting your memory if you are deprived of sleep.

One research, for example, investigated the effects of sleep in 40 children aged between 10 and 14 years.

One group of children were trained in the evening for memory tests, then tested after a night's sleep the next morning. On the same day, the other group was trained and tested, with no sleep between the training and testing.

On memory tests, the group that slept during training and testing performed 20 percent better.

Another study found that nurses who worked the night shift made more mathematical errors and that 68 percent of them scored lower on memory tests than nurses who worked the day shift.

For optimal health, health experts recommend that adults get between seven and nine hours of sleep each evening.

Studies have consistently linked sufficient sleep with better performance in memory. Sleep helps with memory consolidation. If you're well-rested, you're more likely to do better on memory tests than if you're sleep-deprived.

6. Practice mindfulness

Mindfulness is a state of mind in which you concentrate on your present situation and maintain awareness of your surroundings and feelings.

In meditation, mindfulness is used, but the two are not the same. Meditation is a more formal practice, whereas attention is a mental habit that you can use in any situation.

Studies have shown that mindfulness is effective at reducing stress and improving memory and concentration.

One analysis of 293 students in psychology found that those who had been trained in mindfulness had better recognition-memory efficiency when remembering items relative to students who had not undergone carefulness training.

Mindfulness was also linked to a lower risk of age-related cognitive decline and overall psychological wellbeing improvement.

Incorporate mindfulness methods into your everyday life by paying more attention to your current moment, reflecting on your breathing, and gradually resetting your concentration as your mind wanders around.

Practicing mindfulness exercises was correlated with improved output in memory. Mindfulness is also associated with decreased cognitive loss concerning age.

7. Drink Less Alcohol

Consuming too many alcoholic drinks can, in many ways, be harmful to your health and can hurt your memory.

Binge drinking is a drinking pattern that raises alcohol levels in your blood to 0.08 grams per ml or more. Studies have shown that this alters the brain and leads to memory deficits.

A study of 155 freshens college students found that students who consumed six or more drinks within a short period, either weekly or monthly, had problems with immediate and delayed memory-recall tests relative to students who never drank binge.

Alcohol shows neurotoxic brain effects. Repeated binge drinking episodes can damage the hippocampus, a part of the brain that plays an important role in memory.

While it is perfectly healthy to have a drink or two now and then, avoiding excessive alcohol intake is a smart way to protect your memory.

Alcohol has neurotoxic effects on the brain, including a decrease in output in memory. Occasional moderate drinking is not a problem, but binge drinking can damage your hippocampus, a critical memory-related area of your brain.

8. Train the brain

Playing brain games to improve your thinking skills is a fun and successful way to enhance your memory.

Crosswords, word-recall games, Tetris, and even smartphone memory-training applications are great ways to improve memory.

Research involving 42 adults with moderate cognitive disability found that playing games on a brain-training device for eight hours over four weeks improved memory test output.

Another study of 4,715 people showed that their short-term memory, working memory, concentration, and problem-solving improved significantly compared with a control group when they did 15 minutes of an online brain-training program at least five days a week.

Also, brain-training games have been shown to help lower the risk of dementia in older adults.

Games that challenge your brain can help reinforce your memory and reduce the risk of dementia.

9. Cut back on refined Carbohydrates

The ingestion of large quantities of refined carbohydrates, such as cakes, pasta, cookies, white rice, and white bread, will harm your memory.

These foods have a high glycemic index, which means that the body quickly digests these carbohydrates, resulting in a spike in blood sugar levels.

Studies have shown that the Western diet, high in refined carbohydrates, is associated with dementia, cognitive decline, and decreased cognitive function.

One analysis of 317 healthy children showed that those who ate more refined carbohydrates such as white rice, noodles, and fast food had decreased cognitive ability with impaired short-term and working memory.

Another study showed that adults consuming ready-to-eat cereal daily had poorer cognitive function than those consuming cereal less often.

Like added sugar, refined carbohydrates lead to a spike in blood sugar levels that may, over time, damage your brain. Dementia, cognitive impairment, and decreased brain function have been linked with diets high in processed carbohydrates.

10. Have the levels of vitamin D testing

Vitamin D is an important nutrient in the body that plays many vital roles.

Low vitamin D levels have been associated with several health problems, including a decrease in cognitive function.

A five-year study that tracked 318 older adults found that those with blood levels of vitamin D below 20 nanograms per ml lost their memory and other cognitive abilities faster than those with normal levels of vitamin D.

High vitamin D levels were also related to a higher risk of developing dementia.

Vitamin D deficiency is very common, especially in colder climates and darker-skin ones. Speak to your doctor about taking a blood test to find out whether you need a supplement of vitamin D.

Vitamin-D deficiency is very common, particularly in colder climates, and has been associated with cognitive impairment and dementia associated with aging. When you suspect you have insufficient levels of vitamin D, ask your doctor for a blood test.

11. Exercise More

Exercising is important for physical and mental health as a whole.

Research has found it to be beneficial to the brain and can help improve memory in people of all ages, from kids to older adults.

For example, a study of 144 individuals aged 19 to 93 found that a single bout of 15 minutes of moderate exercise on a stationary bike contributed to enhanced cognitive performance across all ages, including memory.

Many studies have shown exercise can increase neuroprotective protein secretion and promote neuronal growth and development, leading to improved brain health.

Daily midlife exercise is also related to a reduced risk of developing dementia later in life.

Exercise brings amazing benefits to your entire body, including your brain. Even moderate exercise has been shown to improve cognitive performance across all age groups, including memory for short periods.

12. Choose Inflammatory foods

Eating a diet rich in anti-inflammatory foods will help your memory improve.

Antioxidants help to minimize inflammation in the body by reducing the oxidative stress that free radicals can cause. Antioxidants can be consumed in foods such as fruit, vegetables, and teas.

A recent study of nine studies of over 31,000 participants showed that those who eat more fruits and vegetables had lower rates of cognitive deterioration and dementia relative to those who consumed less of those healthy foods.

Berries are especially high in antioxidants such as flavonoids and anthocyanins. Eating them can be an excellent way of avoiding memory loss.

One research involving more than 16,000 women found that those who consumed the most blueberries and strawberries had lower levels of cognitive impairment and memory loss than people who eat fewer berries.

Anti-inflammatory foods, especially berries and other foods high in antioxidants, are great for your brain. You can't go wrong with eating a variety of fruits and vegetables to add more anti-inflammatory foods into your diet.

13. Take Curcumin

Curcumin is a compound found in the turmeric plant, at high concentrations. It is one of a compound group, called polyphenols.

It is a powerful antioxidant and exerts strong anti-inflammatory effects within the body.

Multiple animal studies have shown that curcumin decreases brain oxidative damage and inflammation and also reduces the volume of amyloid plaques. These accumulate on neurons and cause death in cells and tissues, leading to loss of memory.

Indeed, the accumulation of amyloid plaque can play a role in the progression of Alzheimer's disease.

Although more human research on the effects of curcumin on memory is required, animal studies indicate that it may be successful in improving memory and preventing cognitive decline.

Curcumin represents a potent antioxidant. Animal studies have demonstrated that it reduces brain inflammation and amyloid plaques. There is, therefore, a need for further human research.

14. Add some coconut to your diet

Cocoa is not only tasty but also nutritious, offering a potent dose of flavonoids called antioxidants. Research suggests that flavonoids are especially good for the brain.

They can help stimulate blood vessel and neuron production, and increase blood flow in memory-involved parts of the brain.

A study of 30 healthy people found that those who consumed dark chocolate with 720 mg of cocoa flavonoids displayed improved memory compared with those who consumed white chocolate without cocoa flavonoids.

Choose dark chocolate with a cocoa content of 70 percent or higher to get the most out of chocolate. That will help ensure that greater quantities of antioxidants such as flavonoids are present in it.

Cocoa is rich in antioxidants, which can help improve performance in memory. Select dark chocolate with 70 percent or higher cacao, so you get a concentrated dose of antioxidants.

The Low Line

There are a lot of interesting, easy, and even tasty ways to make your memory better.

All excellent strategies include improving your mind and body, enjoying a great piece of chocolate, and reducing the amount of added sugar in your diet.

Start adding to your daily routine some of these science-backed tips to improve your brain health and keep your memory in top shape.

Chapter 11: HABITS OF UNLIMITED PERSONAL GROWTH

Our mind is continually thinking, analyzing, and trying to make sense of what is happening at all times and in all situations, but just because we have vast experience with thought doesn't mean that we are experts in our ability to think effectively. This is because a great deal of our thinking is automatic and outside our control. What and how we feel becomes an ingrained habit that has grown all our lives. We adopt values, opinions, and perceptions from society, our families, friends, and the media, which may or may not be valid, and may or may not help us attain our objectives.

Simply put, habits of thought and reactions become a habit that we experience the world with. So beginning to control what we're thinking about and making a strategy to change our thought habits is the first step towards improving our lives for the better. Here are ten useful ways of thought and how to improve them.

Reflect on your feelings

Metacognition, or thinking about thought, helps us to discover our patterns of thinking and how they influence our emotions and behaviors. When we begin to consider our thoughts, with thoughts that empower, encourage, and maintain our goals, we will start to reprogram restricting and belittle thoughts. Learn to think and be mindful of what you are considering. Contemplate what you want to become, and communicate with this picture as if you are this ideal already.

Keep open to lifelong learning

The more I read, the more I remember that I know nothing. There is so much to learn, be it from experience or schooling. The more versed we are in a subject, the higher the growth continues. We are more likely to think creatively with knowledge and build on our current understanding. Explore fascinating new topics, and learn new skills. Create a plan to learn and grow something unique inside your company. I break into social, physical, mental, and spiritual (EPMS) realms my learning and personal development.

Only think flexibly

Being judgmental and unnecessarily critical of ourselves and others is one of the most destructive patterns of thought. You being judgmental leads to being close-minded. Overcome this by the recognition of various views and viewpoints. The aim is to search for different and opposing points of view. Explore them impartially, and suggest new ideas. Adopt ideas which you believe are going to be helpful and which complement your beliefs.

Seeking a sense of humor

Humor is a tool for creative imagination and optimistic emotions. We don't want to get into the trap of being too serious and over-thinking small problems. This can hinder our creativity and ability to make essential choices. In some instances, laughter can be beneficial, which lightens the emotional burden and encourages more positive thought— using humor to cope with tension and anger on times.

Be patient and compassionate

Connecting with others and achieving their level is an ability that demands that we listen to what other people think and feel. This isn't always normal but can be learned for sure. Empathy and empathy come from listening to people at their best. Identify psychological barriers and focus on your inadequate methods to listen and communicate with others. To evolve as a caring individual, we have to desire good things even more for others than we want them for ourselves.

Think about yourself

Don't believe whatever you say, and don't consider whatever you think, at least until you know you want to consider it. It can be hard to think outside the box when we've been told there's a "true" way of doing things our whole lives. We're learning not to challenge things or think critically, and instead, we're going along with the party and accepting what's said at face value. The next time you're disagreeing or hearing your instincts telling you something else, don't be afraid to speak up and stand up. We need to learn to think beyond traditional concepts that are out of fashion to create positive progress in the world and develop as a human being.

Using imagination to construct creativity

Our ingenuity and imagination are among the greatest gifts we have. You could have had an imaginary friend when you were a kid, or you developed your language or any number of imaginary games. Get back in touch with your desire to be creative, and don't let the inclination squelch society. It may feel like we have to "grow up" as we get older, and then we stop dreaming and fantasizing and using your imagination to take up a project for work. Connect this ability through art, music, writing, or speaking, and continue to develop it. Practice invention and make this part of your being known.

Respond with wonder and amazement

Learn to understand life's grand mysteries. It opens our minds when we can find motivation, intention, and sense, and we can see things in a new way. Link to something bigger and be a part of something that makes you feel good and excited about it. Create a list of 5 things that cause wonder, awe, inspiration, or profound gratitude to you. Find these out, and when they arise, be open to those moments.

Take responsibility for risks

As an individual, we must be willing to take healthy risks to develop and evolve. Change is a constant, but the least we can do during those moments is to search for openings. If fear and anxiety run wild, we will cease to develop or move outside our comfort zone. Taking chances needn't be a total gamble. Set targets that are practical and plausible, but which are meaningful as well, and stretch your boundaries. Think bold and heavy, but do have a realistic plan.

Pray and meditate

Developing a daily practice of reflecting on transcendence and spiritual development provides tremendous peace and wisdom. Meditation and meditation are two activities that help us become more conscious of what we think and give us the insight we should integrate into our decision-making process. Abstract and ponder great spiritual teachings and recite these ideas and memorize them. I am going to recommend St Francis of Assisi's prayer. It's a constant method to achieve greater productivity and effectiveness.

A lot of our success and development comes from personal growth and the way we think. Recognize those patterns of thoughts that keep you back, and take time and effort to change your way of thinking.

Chapter 12: SPEED READING MYTHS AND PRACTICE LEVEL

Speed reading consists of several techniques that allow one to read more quickly. This was first used in World War II by the United States Air Force to classify quicker enemy aircraft. The system was later built, in the late 1950s, and in recent years it has attracted quite a several enthusiasts. The appeal is plain to see. Think back when you've done a very interesting and captivating book, and put it down. Wouldn't you want to read more of those in the same period? And maybe you've had enough and just want to finish the dreaded chapter in your book on anatomy.

Speed reading promises all of the above, plus much more. However, in this case, the saying "if it is too good to be true, then possibly it is" fits perfectly. Before you latch on to the idea desperately hoping to shorten your reading sessions, pause for a moment. It's not as good speed reading as enthusiasts say. The quote from Woody Allen may be an overstatement at very high levels of reading. You may also leave out that Russia is engaged in "War and Peace." In reality, you couldn't understand anything. The theory of speed reading and its methods will be explored here. It'll even show you ways to get you to read quickly.

While speed reading and reading fast are quite similar in titles, they are very different in practice.

Myth or reality?

Speed reading is something of a legend. Some clarifications are required before going on further. Ordinary Jane or Joe's average reading pace is 200–300 words per minute. Nevertheless, multiple reading strategies will increase it by up to 500 words per minute (more information later). Although impressive, you're not speed reading at this point; you're only reading quickly. While some professionals claim to achieve, speed reading occurs at speeds of 1000 words per minute. You'd read the typical anatomy book from cover to cover in about 12 hours, to put it into perspective.

It is, therefore, difficult to understand at this reading rate. Simply, the brain can not assimilate information at such a high rate of reading. You look at pages without any idea what the words and phrases are telling you. What is the point of using a method of learning or reading if you are not learning something from it? When after using it, you can't grasp something, you are pretty much on square one. This helped you positively not.

What a myth?

In overcoming two obstacles, science has demystified speed reading: the structure and physiology of the eye itself, and neuronal processing.

Limitations set by the eye

The first obstacle to reading speed is physical-two eyes of your own. How is speed reading so challenging? It all comes down to the way the eyes interpret the written text visually when reading. Although you may think your eyes are traveling continuously along a line, they don't actually. Then, they make quick and very fast moves (saccades) from a fixed point to the next (fixations).

These are similar to a car journeying to its destination and stopping at all the lights.

The saccades are regulated by the frontal eye fields in the frontal cortex and the upper colliculus in the midbrain. Saccades occur because the fovea is extremely small. This pit is the main part of the retina that allows for high resolution viewing. Therefore, to allow you to see something as clearly as possible, the entire area needs to be separated into several points and moved between them.

Visual signals enter the eye during fixations and reach the retina. The fovea is once more the anatomical enemy of speed reading. Only an incredibly small region of 100 percent sharpness (acuity) is seen at moments when the eye is set. The region is closely associated with the vision center and ranges between four and five letters. Acuity decreases as the distance from the central point rises and the fovea. This means you can't properly distinguish the words to read and interpret them. That is like looking through the peephole of your front door.

Limitations to neuronal diagnosis

The knowledge must move through your working memory for understanding to take place. This system is part of the short-term memory that stores retrieve and manipulate information temporarily during cognitive tasks such as listening, reading, and writing. The information must first be translated to a phonological code before it is temporarily processed while reading.

Working memory has a low and limited capacity to bust the truth of reading rates. This cap for reading is of five words (chunks). Essentially, your brain may temporarily remember five words, as long as you don't overwhelm it in a short time with extra details. You overload your working memory if you read fast, and nothing makes sense because you forget what you've just read. In addition to this, this ability is completely at the hands of genetics. In other words, it can't in any way be exceeded, expanded, or educated. It is in a stone setting.

What about all the approaches to speed reading?

It's very mechanical if you look at the reading process discussed above. It still has saccades and fixations to it. Theoretically, you could process more words in the same amount of time by reducing the time spent on each of these measures. So-called speed readers say different techniques or activities have accomplished this.

Removing Sub-vocalisation

You're likely reading this book by silently saying every word in your head. It all started when you first learned to read. Your teacher has told you to read out loud and then, quietly, later. Experts in speed reading claim that if you stop "hearing" or "saying" the words within your brain, you can cut down on time spent on fixations, and you will reach 1000 words per minute. This could be possible, but it is correlated with many problems.

Earlier in this book, it was stated that to access your working memory, sub-vocalization is needed for the details. In other words, to understand, the anatomy and physiology compel you to do so. If you do away with it, you will stop knowing something, and you'd be back to square one. On top of that, mentally, "saying," every word keeps you focused and alert when reading. This is crucial, particularly when dealing with such anatomy as academic and scientific research. Instead of knowing it, you look at a single word, and the entire book turns to gibberish. Certainly not quite a sight when it comes to neuroanatomy!

Rapid Serial Visual Presentation

Digital speed reading systems, such as Spritz, also employ this method. Single words appear at the same location on your phone, preventing saccades. In principle, this sounds possible-you set the target velocity, you get used to it, you increase it, and suddenly you read speed. Not too fast! Remember the limited capacity of your mind working? You can erase the saccades and lower the fixations as much as you like, but it's difficult to flood your working memory with words. It isn't working out.

Reading several lines at a time

Another point about speed reading is that, instead of just one, you can take in more lines per eye fixation. Do you recall the fovea's small scale and its understanding? Your anatomy and physiology once again stop you from reading more than one line in one go. Additionally, there is no experimental research that indicates that the human eye can read many lines at once.

Skimming

Speed readers also say most information is redundant in a line, book, or essay. So if you miss those sections, you'd hit the end faster than reading every single word. This approach involves primarily looking at names, headings, paragraph openings, bold phrases, diagrams, etc. Having an overall image is something of a check. It does have both advantages and disadvantages, however.

Skimming is also important for faster reading (more on that later).

But it's an incomplete step and just a preliminary step. It is similar to creating a map with all the towns and villages but without roads to show how they are all connected. You don't get the whole point of view if you just skim the text. Perhaps worse, you might be constructing the wrong perspective. When it comes to scientific knowledge, including anatomy, this is suicide! Just whisper about the fact that blood is coming back to the heart via the aorta, and you'll know about it!

Exercising speed reading

Speak to a speed reader, and you'll probably learn that using all of the above methods has helped him reach an amazing level of reading. This is true, in fact, but it has a different connotation. It's not speed reading techniques practice that makes you able to read quickly. It's the fact that reading usually helps you to learn more easily with that fluency. This is not a technique for speed reading.

Fluency is the ability to read text with accuracy, speed, and expression. It bridges the awareness of words and their comprehension. Recognition is one key term. The more books that you are exposed to, and the more you read, the more familiar words that you hear become.

Instead of pausing when you hit a word like "verisimilitude," if you have heard it before, you can know it far more easily. In other words, by avoiding the lengthy "ver-i-si-mil-itude," you can waste less time and therefore read faster. Don't even mention the words' anatomy frequency!

How can you read out more quickly?

Hopefully, by now, you're persuaded that speed reading can't be done without losing comprehension. There are, however, people who read faster than others. If the range of reading speed is 100 to 500 words per minute, then this speed can be increased. This is how to:

- Read a lot
- Take off distractions
- Skim first
- Using a mouse pointer

Each of the suggestions above helps you speed up your reading. The magic happens, though, when you try to combine them all. The more you learn, the more you become fluent, and the faster you start learning complicated words. You remove interferences by eliminating distractions that your focus on reading itself. This helps you to focus entirely on a single task and use your working memory to its fullest ability. You get an idea of what the section is about by skimming and searching for relevant details first, and you know what to expect from it.

This does away with the unknown. If you use a compass, rather than wandering about, your eyes and mind are more focused on one level. You can move the pointer a little faster as well, and it's as though your eyes have no choice but to follow it. However, you need to remember that it is a long process to boost your level. You not only wake up one morning with the ability to read 500 words per minute, but with patience and determination, it's certainly doable.

Though they won't help you read your whole book about anatomy in 12 hours, you'll benefit from it. All those posts from Kenhub are going to be a breeze to get through, now that you know how to read quicker. Want to get to know the clavicle? Choose a quiet place free from distractions, click here, skim the book by looking at the headlines, pictures, and bold words and start reading. In a fraction of the time, you will be getting through it. Need an alternative, even faster? Check out the photos! You do not need to read!

Listen to Shakespeare, then, as he says, "All that glitters isn't gold;/ you've always heard this saying, " Speed reading is something of a dream. It can be a fun party trick, but it is useless for the actual reading purposes, so understanding is lost. Fortunately, you can read faster, but reading speed itself is not the shortcut that you were possibly searching for to get through anatomy.

Highlights

- Speed reading is a myth and not as good as enthusiasts believe. The brain actually can not assimilate information at exceptionally high read rates, so if after using it, you can't comprehend something, you're pretty much on square one.
- The fovea between your own two eyes is the anatomical enemy of speed reading. This is like looking through the peephole of your front door. Although you might think that when you are reading, your eyes move continuously along a line, they are not necessarily due to the small size of the fovea. It needs to split the whole region into several points and switch between them for crystal clear vision. Furthermore, the truth of speed reading is beset by the low and restricted power of your working memory, which nature set in stone. If you overload your working memory, there is no point in doing.

- Speed-reading methods are a myth too. Your physiology and anatomy push you to sub-voice and stop you from reading several lines in one go. Your working memory restricts Rapid Serial Visual Representation, and skimming is just a preliminary and incomplete phase.

- By increasing the fluency, removing interferences, skimming, and using a pointer, you can read more easily.

Chapter 13: 5 WAYS CHESS WILL IMPROVE YOUR MIND

Want to make better decisions and turn your brain? Play Chess, a game synonymous with brain strength and intellect. Numerous studies have shown it has improved several mental skills and has increased in popularity around the world.

According to a 2012 YouGov polling report approved by the World-Chess-Federation, 70 percent of adults have played chess at some stage in their lives, with the number of chess players worldwide estimated at over 605 million. The number of participating chess players in the US was 15 percent, in Germany 23 percent, and Russia 43 percent.

A whopping 85 million played chess in India boosted by the success of Viswanathan Anand, the former world chess champion.

Some more recent figures from 2014 World Chess Championship organizers say that 1.2 billion viewers watched the game.

How are you playing Chess? To be brief: it's a board game played by two players, each with 16 pieces, who use strategic thinking to put the opponent's king piece under an attack it can't escape from, called a "checkmate."

Chess is an ancient game dating back at least 1500 years. It probably originated in India, originating from the chaturanga strategy game. Chess went through a variety of ways, but gradually the rules were developed, and in the 19th-century world championships started to take place. Norwegian Magnus Carlsen, who recently defended his title against the Russian Sergey Karjakin, is the reigning world chess champion. Chess champ for women is Chinese Hou Yifan.

It's worth noting that chess champions are also some of the smartest people in the world, with the recent world champion Garry Kasparov, who contributed to Big Think, reportedly having an IQ of 190. In contrast, the female champion Judit Polgar, who became a Grandmaster at 15, has an IQ of 170.

If you wanted to be more convinced here are five reasons why you should find a spot in your life for chess:

1. Chess improves critical thinking capabilities

As a logic-based game that executes various possible combinations of moves at once, it's designed to activate your brain functions. There are a variety of studies showing how chess can boost the powers of thought. One way of doing this is by pattern recognition.

Studies of former world champion Garry Kasparov showed how easily trends understood by a player of his caliber.

It was also shown that successful chess players use both sides of the brain to make decisions, involving the visual information processing portion of the brain to identify patterns, and the analytical side to choose the right logical move.

Many studies illustrate the curious fact that the elite players' brains are generally smaller than the non-experts, likely leading to "localized shrinkage" to maximize neural performance.

2. Chess could make your memory better

Chess is an ideal recall exercise because it promotes the retrieval of actions for various strategic purposes. The better players fill their memories with combinations they can create. The research revealed how the Grandmasters' minds function by tracking thousands of moves.

3. Chess players enjoy success

The YouGov poll in 2012 also established a strong association between becoming a professional chess player and various achievement and success indicators. Successful chess players account for 78 percent of university graduates—20 percent of households who regularly play chess over $120,000. Chess players are five times more likely to read in-depth analyzes and reviews with high brows. We are more expected to be wealthier, more likely to buy luxury goods by 40 percent.

The avid chess player is Peter Thiel, a successful venture capitalist, co-founder of Paypal, and a key figure in the 2016 presidential election.

And amongst the popular, he is not alone. Paul Allen and Bill Gates, the founders of Microsoft, have been known to play one another as do other Silicon Valley titans. Acting legends included lifelong chess players Humphrey Bogart, Lauren Bacall, Marilyn Monroe, and Marlon Brando. This was the case for John Wayne. And it was Stanley
Kubrick who directed nice. Arnold Schwarzenegger, Nicholas Cage, Ray Charles, Ben Affleck, Bono, Will Smith, and Howard Stern are other celebrities known for their chess prowess.

4. Chess will make the children smarter.

Several studies have been done to show that playing chess (in one case for 18 weeks) has improved the children's IQs involved. Other studies show that chess enhances the analytical and critical thinking skills as well as the imagination skills of children at all stages of the school, thereby improving their progress. Chess has also been shown to improve the arithmetic, comprehension, and verbal abilities of children.

5. Chess will sharpen aging brain

The game has been demonstrated to help elderly people from degenerative brain disorders such as Alzheimer's disease and dementia.

And if you're looking for something more fun to merge brain and brawn, you can participate in chessboxing

Chapter 14: FOODS TO IMPROVE YOUR MIND

Let's face it, and meditation can be hard. Dispose of all misplaced thoughts? Just focus on the breath? Sit still for 10 minutes at a time (minimum)? But we are increasingly finding that practicing regular meditation has so many incredible benefits, from helping us become more compassionate to enable us to be more patient, caring, happy, forgiving, and generous. Luckily, there are certain foods that we can begin to integrate into our diets, which can help us achieve the laser concentration that we are searching for when we sit down to meditate. Here are four food groups which we think are the best:

Whole Grains

Start adding more whole (think, ancient) grains into your diet if you are trying to do your mind and body good. And we're not thinking about white bread, rice or pasta, by grains. Whole-wheat pasta, brown rice, whole-grain bread and are better options than typical white types. Still, even better than those are the variety of whole grains that many now refer to as ancient grains, which include steel-cut oats, quinoa, brown rice, millet, amaranth, and wheatberries, just to name a few. What is the value of certain grain types? They take longer to digest, and they reduce the blood sugar spike that is often associated with a high-carbohydrate diet.

A Bonus Added? Ancient grains are rich in B vitamins, which means they work towards promoting proper brain development, reducing stress, and eventually making you feel more zen while you practice your everyday meditation.

Find out the five ancient grains that you can eat now!

Lemon Water

Look no further than lemon water if you are looking for the ideal start to your day and a boost in your meditation practice. Naturally, lemons are rich in vitamins and minerals, especially vitamin C, an antioxidant that strengthens the immune system, protects against cardiovascular disease, and helps prevent cancer.

Similarly, lemons increase vitality and can help change your mood. How? How? All lemons and limes are among the few foods that produce more negative charged ions than positive ones, supplying the body with an energy boost as it reaches the digestive tract. The soothing lemon fragrance has mood-enhancing and energizing properties. Its new, citrusy scent will make your mood lighter and help clear your mind. Being rich in potassium (an essential mineral that acts alongside sodium in the brain and nervous system for smooth electrical transmission), lemons also help to alleviate depression, anxiety, fogginess, and forgetfulness.

Our recommendations? First thing when you wake up and meditate, drink on a glass of lemon water before you sit down.

Whole Fruit & Vegetables

Yeah, one of the best things that you can do for your body is eating a diet rich in whole fruits and vegetables. But have you known to your mind that they are equally powerful? Root vegetables are filled with all kinds of vitamins and minerals, including sweet potatoes, cabbage, and carrots. Nonetheless, beta-carotene has been shown to boost your immune system in these specific veggies to help keep you safe and keep your mind sharp.

They're also chock-full of carbohydrates, meaning they're slow to digest, and you're going to feel full longer. Cauliflower, spinach, eggplant, broccoli, strawberries, kale, raspberries, grapefruit, avocado, blueberries, and pomegranate seeds are all those fruits and vegetables we love right now.

A simple way to make sure you get fresh fruits and vegetables in your daily fix? Combine your favorite grain (we like quinoa or wheatberries) with baby kale or spinach, avocado, pomegranate seeds, and some delicious roasted broccoli or cauliflower to make a big super salad or bowl for lunch or dinner. Drizzle with your favorite dressing (the one based on tahini is super fresh!) and eat right away. We promise you will, in no time, be on your way to a beautifully zen state!

Nuts & Seeds

Nuts and seeds are a very good source of magnesium (along with whole grains and green vegetables) Magnesium is one of the most abundant minerals in our bodies and is essential to our health, but deficiencies are growing despite this. It is currently estimated that 60 percent of us don't get enough magnesium from the food we consume and thus manifest in symptoms such as anxiety, heart arrhythmias, insulin resistance, muscle spasms, and sleep disturbances. Then, it's clear that consuming more magnesium-rich foods can help to alleviate anxiety and relax our minds.

If you're not a fan of raw nuts like almonds, cashews or hazelnuts, why not consider spreading on your morning toast some balanced omega-rich nut butter.

Are you looking for a tasty and quick way to add more nuts to your diet? Why not try one of our nut butter favorites!

So, what things can we stop before we meditate?

Unless you are trying to obey the rules, it is best before you start meditating to avoid all 'tamasic' or 'rajasic' foods. What are you asking? Well, tamasic foods include items like eggs, vinegar, mushrooms, fruit, poultry, fish, etc.

Such foods are thought to produce unclean and wrathful feelings. Rajasic foods include garlic, spicy foods, onions, coffee, tea, soft drinks, and other heavily processed convenience foods with either refined sugar or heavy salt.

However, still, if you're like us and just want to and your everyday anxiety and stress a bit and build a little more zen in your hectic life, our best advice is to eat a balanced diet filled with as many whole foods as possible (read: unprocessed). Limit sugar, processed foods, drink wines, and caffeine in moderation (though we now know that there are many health benefits of both caffeine and alcohol).

THE VALUE OF CHEWING GUM

When are guys chewing gum? If a Mars anthropologist ever visited a typical supermarket, those shelves near the checkout aisle which display dozens of flavored gum options would have puzzled them. The oral version of running on a treadmill sounds like such a stupid habit of chewing without swallowing. And still, for thousands of years, people have been chewing gum, ever since ancient Greeks began popping wads of mastic tree resin in their mouth to sweeten the food. Socrates chewed gum.

It turns out that there is an excellent reason for this long-standing cultural habit: Gum is an important mental output booster that confers all kinds of benefits with no side effects. The most recent gum chewing study came from a team of St. Lawrence University psychologists. The experiment went like this: A battery of challenging cognitive tasks was given to 159 students, such as repeating random numbers backward and solving complex logic puzzles. Half of the subjects chewed the gum (sugar-free and sugar-added), and the other half had little to say.

Here's where things get peculiar: On five out of six studies, those randomly allocated to the gum-chewing condition substantially outperformed those in the control condition.

(One exception was verbal fluency in which participants were asked to name as many words as possible from a given group, such as "animals.") The sugar content of the gum did not influence the output of tests.

Although previous studies have produced similar outcomes – chewing gum is always a better test aid than caffeine – this new study has been studying the gum benefit's time path.

This turned out to be very short-lived, as gum chewers displayed only a performance improvement within the first 20 minutes of testing. Before that, they responded to nonchewers identically.

What responsible for this mental boost? And no one knows. It doesn't seem to rely on glucose, because the same benefits were provided by sugar-free gum. Alternatively, the researchers say that gum improves efficiency due to "mastication-induced anticipation." In other words, the act of chewing awakens us, meaning we are completely focused on the task at hand. That boost is, sadly, temporary. This research's conclusion is straightforward: when you take an exam, save the gum for the toughest part, or when you feel your concentration flagging for certain questions. The gum will help you concentrate, but the relief does not last long.

The new paper adds further to the impressive body of psychological gum literature. Scientists at Coventry University last month noticed that people chewing mint gum experienced a dramatic drop in sleepy feelings. Once tested with the Pupillographic Sleepiness Test (PST), which uses the pupils' oscillations as a measure of tiredness, the participants often appeared less sleepy. We get alertness and concentration when we chew gum but without the jitters.

And then there's that paper, from a Cardiff University researcher. 133 Cognitive experiments were performed with and without the chewing gum. (They were also randomly given gum types, provided with a variety of fruits and mints.) Roughly half of the volunteers were examined when listening to the screeching noise – this was a painful situation – while the other volunteers took the test in a quiet environment. The volunteers rated their mood after each test session and underwent a variety of physiological tests, including heart rate and cortisol levels in the salivary. (Cortisol is a stress hormone, but it is also a good warning indicator.)

Gum chewers, with elevated heart rates and cortisol levels, were more attentive than non-chewers as predicted. We also had reaction times much faster, particularly on more demanding tests. We still seemed in a better mood.

Given the eerie gum force, it seems a little dumb that in the classroom, we don't allow that. (If a pill had the same effects, we would all pop it up.) Of course, the gum is gross and unsightly until it becomes litter. Still, it also tends to be a great stimulant, helping us to enjoy the attentive boost of eating without swallowing or ingesting calories. (Plus, new breath!) A recent review of the literature on gum chewing summarizes the science: "Gum tends to be a functional product with no product."

Reduce pain and anxiety

Would you ever feel better at biting your nails when you're nervous and shaking your legs? Okay, the same idea applies here; nibbling on some gum acts as a great replacement for nervous behaviors instinctually. But don't just take our word for it: participants who chewed gum for 14 days twice a day rated their anxiety substantially less than the non-chewers in a 2011 study, showing higher moods and lower rates of fatigue.

Scientifically speaking, it has been shown that gum chewing can dramatically reduce the cortisol stress hormone, and for most people, the simple chewing act is soothing. Now that's just something to cheer — or chew-on! Find out those other alternative ways of relieving anxiety.

Helps to weight loss

When you are slammed with a case of midday munchies, it may be helpful for your weight-loss regimen to put in some gum over the bag of chips. Not only does this slash the calorie count, but over time the gum can start serving as a "signal," you no longer need to eat. This essentially curbs the cravings and lessens the intake. Health studies suggest that the biggest gain comes from those who reach for a gum stick, rather than snacks between meals.

The mindless nibbling has been shown to help reduce appetite; a study from Rhode Island University has shown that at lunchtime, people who chewed gum ended up eating 67 percent fewer calories than non-gum chewers.

Chapter 15: AEROBIC EXERCISE FOR THE BRAIN

Aerobic exercise reduces the risk of many diseases, from heart disease to dementia. While there are some benefits to all types of physical activity, aerobic exercise is particularly beneficial as it allows the heart and lungs to function harder than normal.

National recommendations on physical activity suggest an aerobic exercise of at least 150 minutes a week.

Some examples of doing aerobics include:

- Running
- Cycling
- Walking
- Swimming
- Aerobics Classes

We address some of the benefits aerobic exercise provides to the body and brain in this book.

Benefits for the body

Aerobic activity helps the body in all manner of ways. Including:

1. Preventing heart attacks

Aerobic activity is important to safeguarding healthy heart, lungs, and blood vessels. Regular aerobic exercise can help prevent heart disease and decrease the risk of death from the condition.

2. Keeping a healthy weight

Sharing the exercise on Pinterest Aerobic will help prevent heart disease and regulate blood sugar levels.

Those who want to lose weight will have to make sure they eat more calories than they consume, leading to a caloric deficit.

Aerobic exercise allows the body to use energy to burn calories. It's a great way to push the body into a caloric deficit, which results in weight loss. But most people would still need to reduce the number of calories they eat to meet a caloric deficit.

3. Controlling blood sugar levels

It is necessary to keep the blood sugar levels under control to reduce the risk of type 2 diabetes. Keeping the blood sugar levels within a safe range is important for people with diabetes. High sugar in the blood can damage the blood vessels and cause heart disease.

Insulin is necessary to control sugar in the blood. Aerobic activity can increase sensitivity to insulin, meaning that the body requires less insulin to regulate blood sugar levels.

The muscles also draw glucose from the blood during exercise. Exercising, therefore, helps avoid too high blood sugar levels from increasing.

4. Reduces blood pressure

High blood pressure puts stress on the heart and blood vessels. This can have significant effects over time, such as can the likelihood of a heart attack or stroke.

Aerobic exercise can help maintain good blood pressure. A study of 391 studies in the British Journal of Sports Medicine found exercise to be as effective in lowering high blood pressure as blood pressure drugs.

5. Prevent and control stroke

A stroke occurs when blood flow to a brain region is clogged. It can have serious consequences, even life-threatening. By keeping the blood vessels and the heart safe, routine aerobic exercise decreases the risk of a stroke.

It's also crucial to remain as involved as possible for people who have had a stroke to help rehabilitation and the possibility of another stroke. A doctor may advise an individual on how best to build up strength after a stroke and start exercising again.

6. Greater lifespan

Aerobic activity has such a wide variety of benefits to wellness that it helps people live longer. Higher levels of aerobic activity, regardless of the exercise duration, raising the risk of death.

7. Enhance physical activity

The ability to perform daily living tasks is vital for the preservation of independence and health. Aerobic exercise strengthens the physical capacities that a person needs to work daily. Physical exercise also helps to avoid accidents and injuries that occur.

Good for the brain

The brain also benefits from aerobic exercise in the following ways:

1. Reducing dementia threats

Regular aerobic exercise, the most common cause of dementia, is one of the most effective ways of avoiding Alzheimer's disease.

Evidence has shown that the likelihood of cognitive impairment and dementia is lower for individuals with higher rates of physical activity.

2. Helps with Depression Symptoms and Anxiety

Several clinical trials have shown that aerobic activity in people with depression and anxiety disorders decreases the symptoms. Aerobic exercise also increases physical health and can help to prevent depression and anxiety disorders from arising.

3. Enhancing cognitive performance

Although aerobic exercise can delay cognitive impairment in later life, it can also improve child and adolescent thought processes.

Several studies have found evidence to indicate that aerobic activity and physical health have ties to better school grades and enhanced cognitive task performance, such as memory tests.

4. Improving mental wellbeing

Aerobic exercise is responsible for many biological processes that help brain function. A recent review article's authors concluded that the aerobic exercise could:

- Improve the size and function of main brain regions like the hippocampus
- Help brain regulation reactions to stress
- Reduces inflammation

- Raising oxidative stress resistance

These improvements are likely to lead to the mental health and memory benefits of exercise.

Chapter 16: THE POWER OF NEGATIVE THINKING AND THE WAY IT CAN BE REVERSED

*   Brain effects: Memory is impaired. Information processing is slowed down. The Amygdala, which governs the answer to the fight or flight, gets uncontrolled. If a stressful circumstance happens, the Amygdala can not determine if it is a condition of life or death or an irritation. The effect is then an overreaction to any unpleasant situation, whether it's a mild inconvenience or a real traumatic incident. This can lead to a dangerous situation or an inability to cope with some form of stress.

*   Depression: Depression not only affects the mind, but it can also cause physical damage, constant joint discomfort, discomfort in the arm/leg, and changes in appetite. Sleep sometimes gets interrupted. It's reducing your immune function. Untreated left, depression may lead to other mood disorders, or exacerbate them.

*   loneliness: If anyone is known to be a chronic negative person, they do not have a large circle of friends. Most people tend to steer clear of negativity and not pull them down to find friends who raise them. This isolation can also lead to depressive feelings.

*   Job Instability: People who are pessimistic thinkers do not want to try hard at work, or may give up because they don't think a problem can be solved. Employers want people ready to do whatever it takes to get a job done so that negative thinking is not a marketable ability. This can show up as early as an interview, so it could be challenging for those pessimistic thoughts to get some kind of professional role.

*   Relationship Issues: Individuals want a life partner who is there to speak to and get input from them. They want to lean on someone who is a shoulder, a cheerleader, and a problem solver. If someone has developed a pessimistic attitude, a long-term relationship can be difficult to maintain. Issues are bound to come up, and you will need to be able to see someone else's angle or look for positive ways to help the other person fix their dilemma.

*   Bodily Consequences: Capacity declines with anger. Thinking one 's appearance is less attractive will influence how you feel for yourself, not paying attention to physical appearance. A radical adverse reaction can also lead to eating problems, ranging from not eating enough to over-eating extremes.

This is not to suggest that they have no negative thoughts or emotions in their lives. No one lives with only optimistic, happy feelings. It is when there is chronic, long-term, and repeated negative thinking that problems will arise.

Reversing it

The brain could have been wired to think pessimistic thoughts, so it should be rewired to think positively. It takes about 21 days to get entrenched with a habit, so completing any of the following tasks may cause you to think positively in 3 weeks.

*   Gratitude Journal: Writing 3-5 items that you appreciate every day will give you a big positive boost. There's nothing enormous or earth-shaking to be. In reality, writing about the little stuff can have a more significant impact on your daily attitude as it is those little things that add up to the big things in life. Buy yourself a journal just for that reason to be inspired to do this every day. It could be a diary, a particular newspaper, or a phone app. Only make sure you do it every day to produce the best result.

*   Journaling: Writing down your thoughts and emotions will help you track your patterns of thought. It can also open your mind to understanding why you have the thoughts you have. You can write openly or buy a newspaper that will inspire you to think about writing about it. Writing and re-reading your thoughts will help you articulate yourself, and maybe break the negative thinking cycle.

*   Random acts of kindness: You will find a plethora of kindness-type tasks while looking online. Typically they come in the form of a calendar containing a random act of kindness which you can do every day. They needn't be extraordinary deeds. As the journal of appreciation, the little things are things that can have the most significant effect. These kind deeds will come back into your life as good karma.

*   Meditation: Meditation shouldn't be a long process. Even 5 minutes of meditation will make your soul and mentality feel good. In meditation, it's not about controlling your mind, so you don't think about anything; it's not about letting your mind dominate you. A lot of podcasts and applications will help you concentrate on being present. You will feel lighter and more optimistic after you meditate. Begin the day with this routine, and you can face everything that comes your way.

Spirituality: Spirituality can take various forms. Some people may feel a powerful pull toward a particular organized religion. Others can feel a connection to a higher force that is not "God." Neither of these alternatives is the right choice or the wrong choice. Having a spiritual tradition gives many people the confidence that they can rely on and transform to something greater than themselves in moments of sorrow, pain, misery, or difficulty. It puts a lot of people in a reasonable mind frame where they believe as they can cope with any problem that occurs.

*   breathing techniques: Breathing exercises will decrease the heart rate, making you less nervous and tense. You have a more optimistic state of mind when you are growing fear and stress. Relevant relaxation exercises will help you stay right now and your concern so you can manage the present situation.

*   Yoga: We are prepared to be healthy and positive beings upon this world. When negative thoughts invade our minds regularly, they make us unbalanced. Even our physical bodies can get unstable. You are calming your body and mind as you start a yoga session. You are advised to remain in the present moment while you practice yoga and to think about why you are there and what you want to get out of the practice at the time. Entering into a yoga practice would have a contented and relaxing effect on all participants.

*   Remove Negative Thoughts: If you can not rid yourself of all negative thoughts, strive to remove them with a positive thought. Stop yourself when a negative thought pops up and substitute the thought with something constructive. For example,

if you have a big job to do, instead of thinking, "I'm never going to finish this," you say, "I'm going to break this down into smaller pieces and get it done."

Chapter 17: PRACTICE MAKES PERFECT:

MUSCLE MEMORY AND "BRAIN TRAINING"

Certainly, repetition and practice are crucial for performance and ultimately for progress when learning to play an instrument or perform a particular pose in yoga class. Athletes train their muscles to recall specific moves so that they can perform at extremely high rates while performing without ever giving mechanics a thought. Likewise, even under the stresses of playing at Carnegie Hall, a concert pianist or violinist may direct their hands along with the keyboard or cords.

A recent article by Doug Lemov in the Wall Street Journal addressed the effectiveness of the rehearsing behaviors typically conducted at a given job to free the brain for other more complex tasks. As the author suggests, in business, medicine, and other technically demanding careers, there are boundless opportunities for this form of "brain-training."

The adage of "see one, do one, teach one" in medicine has become the standard for educating young medical students and physicists.

Within our current program, many hands-on skills were acquired through the years of preparation. Practicing one task until it is almost automatic, as Mr. Lemov explains in his WSJ post, helps us to commit more of our brainpower to other more complex tasks. Practicing skills not only enables us to develop at a specific movement but also, more importantly, allows us to respond easily, calmly, and automatically to a particular situation. In medical practice, this can be a life-saving proposition, particularly in emergencies. I think that in medicine, to apply these concepts more thoroughly, we should strengthen the adage and adapt it to "see one, do others, teach others."

A recent New York Times article identified "brain training" strategies that are being marketed to children aged 11 to 21. Like conventional tutoring, these courses concentrate on brain drills in the face of obstacles, such as number retrieval, sequence memorization, and visual handling tasks. "Brain training" is intended to help students concentrate on complex mental tasks in the face of major auditory and visual stimuli, similar to doing repetitive mechanical activities before they are second.

The idea behind the mechanism is that we can sharpen and brighten the abilities of the brain by doing mental exercises – similar to how a professional golfer will refine his or her golf swing.

I conclude that medical education can very well benefit from integrating these forms of mechanical and cognitive practice sessions into physician preparation. Today, medical centers are beginning to use simulators to train members of the surgery to perform procedures. Doctors in training will continue with the use of simulators to improve muscle memory – then transfer to assist and perform actual surgical procedures to refine their skills.

Simulators do not replace the experience gained in the operating room but can improve protection and expose trainees to further learning opportunities. Also, the interactions between doctor and patient may be replicated and performed using actors as patients.

Many medical schools also use virtual patients to test patient interaction skills. I benefitted tremendously from working with virtual patients in my medical school studies at Wake Forest University. Not only did I learn how to conduct a history and physical examination, but I was also provided with direct input from the patient – I learned the importance of making eye contact, communicating empathy, and forming a bond with the patient in a brief encounter with the examination room.

Inputting far greater focus on "practicing" such interpersonal scenarios, doctors in training would be better prepared to cope with difficult circumstances such as delivering bad news, upset families, or other demanding patient encounters. Perhaps significantly, by incorporating both physical and emotional "work," in very stressful circumstances and conditions like the trauma suite in the emergency department or the operating room, we can operate at extremely high levels.

Practice makes sports, music, and medicine just fine. When medicine becomes more complicated, and new technologies are made available, physicians need to be able to become professional and be able to treat patients under pressure. Also, the relationship between doctor and patient is crucial to the performance. Doctors need to continually work on enhancing our ability to communicate with patients. Although practice will not always make us good, it does make us better doctors and eventually help improve patient outcomes.

UNDERSTANDING WILLINGNESS TO LEARN
What's the will to learn?

It reflects the human appetite, consenting joyfully, or willingness to learn new things and better yourself.

The desire to learn in the business field means you are a person who wants to be more knowledgeable and who wants to be up-to-date with changes and developments in your professional area. You have the drive and the enthusiasm to develop your skills and competencies.

Learning willingness is one of the most important skills nowadays needed by businesses.

Putting on a resume is among the most important skills. And, if you're a person looking for ways to better yourself, please don't hesitate to mention this during the job interview.

Education is a long-lived process, and the experience you have never suffices. There's still something to learn. The desire to learn is one of the best features a person might possess.

Possessing the ability to know has a large number of advantages. Here's their most significant one:

The Importance of Education Will:

- Gives you imaginative power.
- The more things that you know, the more fresh thoughts that come to mind. The willingness to invent requires a much-learned desire.
- Open the doors to career success and business growth.
- If you are stuck with the old stuff, there's no way you can be successful.
- Help deal with unforeseen circumstances.

One of the most critical qualities you need to cope with challenges effectively is getting motivation and a willingness to learn. This will help you find out how to fix the problems.

- Help the self-confidence boost.
- Provides more options for you.

How to make you more likely to learn skills

There is a need to be constantly learning because of the constantly evolving nature of the market to excel in your career.

Everyone must be ready to know. Yet it is a must for businessmen, executives, and leaders!

Have you got a spirit and a will to learn? Do you just want to know someone?

Let's see which are the best tips for boosting your ability to learn the skills:

- Note that the ability to know is always the road to making your dreams come true. Do it every single day yourself. If you want to be competitive, you need to be up to date!

- Meet people inspired by it. It's very important to surround yourself with highintelligent well-educated people to be able to learn from them. All of us know someone who has a good career, and a desire to learn drives him.
- Be open to counseling! Check and ask for other people's views, who are knowledgeable in the field you want to create. Follow their opinions closely.
There's a lot to know from people who are highly educated and knowledgeable.
- Write stories about those who excel. There's a lot you can know from their practice. Hearing about someone who was born poor but who went on to do wonders is so inspired.

- Don't be afraid to struggle. Know from that place. A lot of people learn a lot, then struggle, then get scared and then stop learning. It is a mistake! Early or later, all of us end up with disappointment. Find the loss as a means of discovering more new things. Render the loss an encouragement to excel and not an excuse to give up.
- Find out what your shortcomings and deficiencies are in the area that you are looking to grow. When people know what the holes are, they want to fill them up! List all of your shortcomings, and find ways to overcome them.

You have to be able to take risks of winning!

Where to show a desire to learn?

You must be prepared to demonstrate a clear willingness to learn skills while you are going to a work interview and applying for a job position where the ability to learn is among the most valuable skills.

When can you get this done? Here are some helpful tips that you might use during the interview:

How to have your desire to learn revealed. Hint

- Use correct phrases and sentences. Examples: "I'm interested in learning more about marketing research and the tools needed to do it," "I've always been interested in business analysis issues, and I want to develop my experience and expertise in this sector with work in this area."
- Exhibit anticipation. Say those sentences with a smile and excitement! Also, seek to incorporate your attitude during the interview!

- Ask for continuing education. If you lack experience in a specific field, or if your career is in the beginning, demonstrate an interest in improving your skills and expertise.

Ask about continuing education and growth. It demonstrates the desire to know.

People who hire for jobs are looking for fast learners who can adapt quickly to the culture and needs of the business, so always find ways to chat about how you want to learn.

Nowadays, formal education and qualifications are highly necessary. But they just aren't enough! There are also more ways to expand your expertise and develop the skills your profession or company needs!

You just need the drive to know! It can optimize your potential; it can lead to inconceivable results.

Chapter 18: TIPS ON IMPROVING NEGATIVE THINKING

In social and success contexts, pessimistic thinking leads to anxiety. Some social anxiety treatments include a component devoted to converting negative thinking patterns into more effective and constructive ways of looking at circumstances.

The secret to overcoming your negative thoughts is knowing how you think now (and the issues that result) and then using techniques to alter your thoughts or make them have less impact. These steps are usually done with a therapist, but they can also be used as part of a self-help plan to resolve social anxiety.

Understand your way of thinking

One of the first steps in shifting the habits of negative thought is to realize precisely how you think right now. For example, if you choose to see yourself in any situation as complete success or failure, then you're engaging in "black-and-white" thinking. Such negative forms of thought include jumping to conclusions, catastrophic, an overgeneralization.

The habits of unhelpful thought vary in subtle ways. But they all include factual contradictions and contradictory ways of looking at circumstances and individuals.

Learn How to Avoid negative thinking

Cognitive rehabilitation is one of the main aspects of a recovery plan involving cognitive-behavioral therapy (CBT). This method helps you identify and turn negative thinking into more effective and adaptive responses ...

Cognitive restructuring, whether performed in therapy or on your own, requires a stepby-step procedure by which negative thoughts are detected, tested for accuracy, and then substituted. Though it's hard to think at first in this new style, with time and with practice, constructive and logical thoughts can come more naturally.

Coping with criticism

Besides cognitive rehabilitation, another component of CBT that is often beneficial includes something known as "assertive self-defense." Because sometimes people can be harmful and judgmental towards you, it is crucial that you can cope with rejection and criticism.

Typically this phase is performed in therapy with a simulated interaction between you and your therapist to build up your assertiveness skills and assertive critical responses.
These skills are then transferred through homework assignments into the real world.

Practice Mindfulness

Meditation has its origins in mindfulness. It is the art of detaching and seeing yourself from your feelings and emotions as an outside observer.

You can learn how to perceive your thoughts and emotions as objects floating by you during the mindfulness training that you can pause and watch, or let go of. The purpose of being aware is to gain control of your emotional responses to circumstances by allowing your brain's thought component to take over.

Avoid Thought Stopping

Stopping thought is the opposite of being conscious. It's the act of looking for negative thoughts and ensuring they're gone.

The problem with stopping thinking is that the harder you try to suppress the negative thoughts, the more they are going to emerge. Mindfulness is better, as it gives your emotions less weight and reduces the effect they have on you. Stopping thinking might seem to help in the short term, but over time it contributes to more significant anxiety.

Using Thought Journal

Think diaries, also called pension records, can be used to alter negative thinking as part of any process. Think journals help you recognize negative thinking patterns and gain a deeper understanding of how your emotions affect your emotional responses (and not the circumstances you're in). Many CBT recovery programs may include using a thinking diary as part of daily tasks to the homework.

For example, a thought diary entry could break down a person's thinking process on a day, and the emotional and physical reactions resulting from negative thinking patterns. You should substitute irrational feelings about rejection with more constructive and optimistic ways of thinking by the end of the thought test.

If you are dealing with unhealthy habits of thinking, and it impacts your life, consider talking to a mental health professional.

Although sharing your feelings with others can be difficult, therapists can evaluate your negative thinking habits and help you develop a healthy inner dialogue.

Notice that often, many negative thoughts come from two directions. The first is to focus on the past — maybe you ruminate about mistakes, issues, remorse, and everything that hasn't gone the way you thought it should have gone. The second is thinking about the future — fearing what could or may not happen to you, others, or the world.

This can take the form of uncertainty about whether or not you're going to accomplish those goals or worry about your finances or relationship security. Or you might be thinking about getting older. Whatever the specific negative thoughts are, remember that the mind needs to concentrate more on past or future to indulge in negative thinking patterns. Either that or in the present moment, we judge and psychologically mark stuff to be 'evil.'

Chapter 19: CONCLUSION

A perfect way to help you learn more is to read out loud while you're reading. Reading the words out loud rather than just reading them to yourself means you are creating a more clear memory of the details, which will ensure you can remember the facts more readily later. Not only that, but reading out loud means you're not going to lose your concentration and instantly remember that you haven't read at all, but just start at the text! The act of reading the information and then translating it into expression will make it easier to concentrate on the text, and reading out loud will slow the pace a little bit anyway, so you should be given the time to concentrate on what you are reading.

Lastly, reading out loud may help you better understand the points posed in the text. Even if you're reading to yourself in silence, even when a sentence or paragraph after a few readings don't make any sense, you'll always read it aloud to try to understand it better. Reading the whole time loud will help you absorb information more quickly, and make sense of it for future reference.

When you're learning or practicing, memory enhancement can be a great way to improve your study.

It's important to ensure that you remember the knowledge you gain during your course or class for years to come because you don't want to forget it all the minute you finish your final evaluation or walk the class out for the last time.

Techniques such as those mentioned above will not only help boost your memory in general but also allow you to recall the details that you have worked so hard to learn and understand while studying. Both these strategies can be worked on in the way you are learning, so don't worry about wasting extra time doing so. When you work them into your everyday routine, you'll boost your memory in no time, without even thinking about it!